# HIRE POWER

## THE ULTIMATE JOB GUIDE FOR YOUNG CANADIANS

Karen Schaffer

Prentice Hall Canada Inc., Scarborough, Ontario

For Martha, who told me the truth.

**Canadian Cataloguing in Publication Data**

Schaffer, Karen, 1971–
Hire Power : the ultimate job guide for young Canadians

Includes bibliographical references.
ISBN 0-13-742784-0

1. Vocational guidance. 2. Occupations. 3. Job hunting.
I. Title.

HF5381.S32 1997 331.7'02 C97-930387-7



Prentice-Hall, Inc., Upper Saddle River, New Jersey
Prentice-Hall International (UK) Limited, London
Prentice-Hall of Australia, Pty. Limited, Sydney
Prentice-Hall Hispanoamericana, S.A., Mexico City
Prentice-Hall of India Private Limited, New Delhi
Prentice-Hall of Japan, Inc., Tokyo
Simon & Schuster Southeast Asia Private Limited, Singapore
Editora Prentice-Hall do Brasil, Ltda., Rio de Janeiro

ISBN 0-13-742784-0

Managing Editor: Robert Harris
Acquisitions Editor: Sara Borins
Production Editor: Mary Ann McCutcheon
Copy Editor: Karen Alliston
Editorial Assistant: Susanne Frame
Production Coordinator: Julie Preston
Art Director: Mary Opper
Cover and Interior Design: Alex Li
Cover Image: Photo disk, object series #2, image #OS02097
Illustrations: Craig Francis
Page Layout: April Haisell

2 3 4 5 RRD 01 00 99 98 97

Printed and bound in United States

# ACKNOWLEDGMENTS

Thank you to:

Karen Alliston, my editor, for laughing in all the right places and "getting it" without me having to explain, and for letting me wax poetic on love (both in and out of context) when we should have been talking business;

Nicole Bakhit, my researcher, for enduring extra months of work and any number of emergencies—you are my saviour! (thank god you're also a fellow procrastinator);

Sara Borins (my "in" to Prentice Hall) for lighting the way and carrying my project safely to just before the finish line—the lap of victory belongs to you too;

Craig Francis for three years worth of patience and for the way your drawings capture precisely what I'm saying, and then some;

Robert Harris, who took this wacky project in stride; Susanne Frame, the grooviest helping hand an author could want; and everyone at Prentice Hall who were dolphins instead of sharks—thanks for your dedication even before I told you what the book was about;

Thecla Sweeney for believing me that night in Santerini, when I said I could write the book, Alannah Weston for her writer's solidarity and afternoon phone calls that remind me I still know my pop culture, Bruce Sellery for the flowers and for pushing me to much-needed breakthroughs (and Tammy and Kurt too for the much-needed Algonquin trip where Author became Wood Girl), Gord Ray for his fabulous photo shoot that made me feel like a model for an hour, Shawn Labron, for keeping a roof over my head and DKNY on my body. Michelle King for her banana bread, Karina Miller for her baking and long distance love, Natalie LeClair for telling me "just to go finish it," my Grandma for making me get my teeth cleaned when I thought I was too busy, and all my friends and relatives who've given me the extra push, shove and love that I needed along the way;

Chelsea for always wanting to sleep on my lap when I was trying to write;

George Lucas (and his assistant Anne) who wrote me back when I had my first blow as a writer, and got me over my writer's block;

Ian Cameron and Jim Hayhurst of the late Hayhurst Career Centre, who taught me how to write a résumé, make a cold call, and be myself no matter what mountain I faced;

Phyllis Greenberg, who taught me that drama and life go hand in hand; and the Havergal College Guidance Department, who believed in my ability to teach this stuff before I had a contract to prove it;

Landmark Education and the support of my Forum, Advanced and especially Seminar community, that both encouraged me to let go of my stories around finishing this book and gave me the language to explain what I've been trying to say all along;

All the generous students and employers who've given me input over the years and at the very last minute; every one of you taught me something . . . sorry for not putting all your names here. Just know that you walk with my eternal gratitude and if you want me to sign the book "It's only because of you this book got written," bring on over a copy;

The staff from the Youth Employment Centre on Yonge in the summer of '96 who were incredibly generous with their time, input, and experience;

Jason Beck, who returned a favour a hundredfold;

Lloyd Gilbert, who has been through this before and knows more than anyone what this book represents to me;

Malcolm Lester for patiently supporting me year after year when I thought I wasn't ready, and Shelagh Roberts for being the one who understands that it takes longer than you think;

Jen, Chet and Dee for being so patient about my constantly changing schedule so that I could write, and who put my needs first, and also to Derek, Lisa, Jim, Len, Ruby and the rest of my video store co-workers who made working retail for peanuts a bearable thing, and to Lucky for those great sandwiches;

Martha McGrath, my roommate and co-writer in crime—may your dreams come true because you made mine; it's been a pleasure living with you;

Mom for four years of clippings, cards, phone calls and unconditional love, and Rob Higden for saying the infinitely simple sentence "Why don't you write it?";

To all the people in my life who empower me to be this person I want to be . . . thank you forever.

# CONTENTS

PART 1

# PUT THE POWER OF HIRING IN YOUR HANDS

CHAPTER 1

# So You Wanna Get a Job . . .

Okay all you brilliant brainiacs out there, you Mozart-like piano playing prodigies, you twelve-year-old stockbrokers, you eight-year-old organizers of important charity events on the cover of *People* magazine . . . congratulations on your successes. But stop reading, this book is not for you. Yes Doogie, you can go back to the operating table and install that heart valve 'cause this book's for the rest of us. That includes:

- high school students who want their first job, *any* job
- students of any type who want to make some money
- students who have to start defining some kind of future career (for fear of being labelled as one of those mystical Gen-X alternative band types who never shower and will never amount to anything according to parents all over the world)
- students who want the cutting edge in the employment search, to land a decent job, and to learn a few important tips along the way
- those who want to glimpse a bit of the future and see the difference between the job market their parents faced and what *everyone* is encountering today.

If you fall into any of these categories, this book is for you.

# So You Wanna Get a Job, Normal Person . . .

Now you might say, "I just want a job and the doughnut store is hiring." This book is not meant to hold you back from an exciting career in the fine pastry business, if that's what you desire. Just keep reading while you squirt in that jelly. I have a friend who's bright and funny and has planted trees for six years in a row. When she looks for work for the rest of the year I encourage her to come to me for help. "But Karen," she says, "I just want a job. Any job. I'm not picky." The truth is, she's very picky. She won't take a job that will require her to wear "adult" clothes, or that goes against her beliefs as an environmentalist and punk rock girl. And I believe that the more she understands her specific skills, her beliefs, and her needs as an employee, the better her chances are both for getting a job and for the further bonus of—believe it or not—being happy at it.

The key here is that whoever you are, even though you may not have one awe-inspiring, larger-than-an-elephant talent, I *know* you have enough skills to get you a job. How do I know? Because those skills are you. You take them everywhere you go, and you bring them to every job you've had or will have. If I were sitting with you for about an hour I could tell you directly what those skills are, but since I'm not right there, you'll have to trust me. Read the book, and I'll help you find them.

Why are your skills so hard to find? Because they're so much a part of you that you don't even think they exist. Let me tell you another story. A recently graduated student came to see me about a résumé. He'd had several jobs, but to him they were all about making money and having a good time, something he couldn't put on a résumé. He felt pretty discouraged. But buried at the back in a list of other things was a little note: "Organized Fraternity Juvenile Diabetes Event." I asked, "How did that go?" He brushed it off, saying it was no big deal. I persisted and he said, "Oh, we raised five or six thousand dollars." That seemed like a pretty large sum to me, so I asked what had been raised in previous years. "Oh, I don't know, nearly a thousand dollars." Nearly a thousand dollars! "Do you mean to tell me that you sextupled the amount of money raised in previous years?" "Yes," he replied, "I guess I did." So I asked him how he did that. Slowly it came together that he had changed the venue, made the event a toga Bowl-a-Thon party (who could resist bowling in sheets?), and found sponsors that offered prizes, which greatly increased the number of participants and pledges. I asked him if he realized how great a skill it is to be able to organize an event that has such tangible results. He stopped and thought, and then said "You know, I'm always organizing stuff like that. When all my friends wanted to go to a ski chalet for New Year's I organized it. I never think about it but I'm always doing that kind of thing." A Breakthrough! Needless to say, in his résumé we emphasized his amazing ability to organize events and make them fun for others.

## The Job Market of the Future

Our parents came from a generation that had been taught the lessons of the Great Depression. They learned that security, security, and did I mention security? was number one, and that once you had a job, and a job title, and as long as you worked hard, you could keep that job for thirty years. And that was in fact possible, because the economy was such that employers and companies could employ more people while keeping you on.

But today no one's, and I mean no one's, job is absolute. I know a student who wants to work in theatre for a living, and is perfectly willing to take unpaid Joe jobs to earn the experience. This makes her family nervous, since everyone knows how unstable the theatre world is. Different members of the family have suggested that she take her drama skills and become a teacher. Now as well-meaning as the suggestion is, the irony is that right now even trained teachers are finding it incredibly difficult to get a job. A position was recently posted in a Toronto paper for a joint Junior/Senior Kindergarten class. That job had 450 over-qualified people apply. Where's the security there? The problem is that teaching is still a field that we *conceive* of as safe, which is just not true. This is also not to mention that our particular student would have been bored to tears as a teacher. Further, she would have sacrificed her considerable talents and personal growth in the name of the elusive trap of safety. Let's get the people who really *want* to teach in the classrooms.

I believe, and research backs me up, that jobs and careers are changing rapidly into a much more flexible, adaptable, and less describable form. Some jobs are becoming scarce, some are booming. More people are working from home, and on their own schedules. And many more people are doing what's called contract work, which means that they're hired for a specific project, for a certain amount of time.

Employers' expectations are changing too. They're beginning to focus on potential employees' reoccurring skills, rather than on their job histories. Now that there's much more competition for jobs, even traditional businesses need to know more about you than just your degree or diploma and your list of previously held jobs. They want to know how you handle certain situations (when customers complain, are you firm, unreasonable, do you follow up with reasons for the problem, do you offer options?) and who you are in the most basic sense.

Finally, part of the reason why those so-called baby boomers are so stressed is because the traditional hierarchical system of management can't sustain itself if everyone is out for individual gain. Management is beginning to take a team-oriented approach—an "everyone is in this together" approach—in order to focus on the job at hand, and not on who's the most important. This means knowing how to speak up for yourself and how to participate as part of a community.

The working world of the turning century is not the same one that was faced by our parents, or even by people fifteen years older than us—the possibility for something new, different, and way more exciting stands in its place. And we get to work there.

## How Does All This Apply to You?

It sounds pretty scary out there if no one's secure, right? But there are advantages to it. It means that we as the younger generation have the ability to try all different kinds of work, since we'll be less tied down to the traditional concept of a career, and we'll have learned to be more flexible in our job situation. Most of us, according to current statistics, will have not one but four different career changes in our lifetimes. I encourage you to take the time to find out what you really want to do, because that's the secret to the job force of the future: knowing what your innate skills are (usually what you love doing anyway) and finding the job that most fits with these skills. Sound like common sense? Maybe now it does, but in the past what we were encouraged to do was take the safe route, regardless of what we loved. We're now coming to the realization that if you do what you love it *is* the safest route, because that's what you'll do the most passionately. If you can figure out your passion (even if it takes a lifetime) I guarantee that you'll be a success at whatever you do.

When I first began to use "adult" job search skills I had just turned eighteen. The summer was fast approaching and I wanted to work in film. I had this fabulous idea that, what with my scintillating drama skills, my dreams of being a Hollywood producer and director were all just a matter of me getting a job as a production assistant on a film. I went to a career centre in Toronto to get some advice, particularly because I hadn't the faintest clue how to get this mythical job, let alone what kind of work the position would entail. I think my career counsellor knew this, and he gently suggested that maybe I'd prefer "running the show," so to speak, as the Head of Drama at a camp. He knew my personality well enough to know that I'd want to be more than just the coffee gal who views the real work from the sidelines. I thought this change of direction was a good one (I *do* like running the show), and he helped me work out what I would say when I called up camp directors to find out about a job.

This was all fine and dandy until I was all alone in a room with a telephone and my messy sheaf of notes. I felt like the biggest dork during the first few calls as I hastily chimed out my little prepared speech. As soon as I finally slowed down and put some breathing space between my words, I felt as though I was reciting a magic spell. Whether the camp director could hire me or not, I got an enthusiastic response from most of them, and some even asked for my résumé for their files for next year. When I finally got the big "yes" from one camp, the director told me I was the youngest person ever to be Head of Drama at that camp. He chose me over someone older and more experienced.

The difference? I knew *who* I was, *what* my skills were, and *how they applied* to the job. To put it simply, I presented myself clearly so that he could be sure of hiring me. These job search techniques weren't really magic on my part. We'll get to them later and you'll see. You can learn them too, and use them to shoot for the job that best fulfills *your* personal goals for the summer.

It can be hard to get a job. Make it easy on yourself. Practise the stuff that follows in this book in order to prepare, not only for the job you want this summer, but for the jobs you'll *really* want for the rest of your life.

## Summer Goals (or I'm in It for the Money)

This is a good time to stop and ask yourself the question, "What are my goals for the summer?" List below the things that come to mind.

1. ______________________________

2. ______________________________

3. ______________________________

4. ______________________________

5. ______________________________

## An Ode to Cold Cash

Okay, let's get down to the real matter at hand. I can muse all I like about happiness, skills, and career opportunities, but the truth of the matter is that many of us would never get a job if we didn't need the money. Hence I expect that many of you put money as number one, or that it at least appeared on your list somewhere. If it didn't, or if you put it there because you thought you should, you probably don't really need a job like the rest of us. And that's okay. Hallelujah if Lotto 649 came through or if your parents are willing to hand out no-strings cash. We don't all get that chance and we'd like you to use it wisely.

I say this because unless the job is really good, you probably won't pursue it wholeheartedly if you don't feel the hunger for the cash. Case in point: one student I know had been stimulated by an Outward Bound adventure the summer before, and decided that not only could she handle tree planting, she'd naturally *love* every minute of it. Our gal came to the interview armed with the line she heard could get her hired: "I need money—BAD!!" The tree-planting boss assumed that she'd be motivated to work like a dog and plant trees from sun up to sun down (which is what tree planters do). The truth is, however, that our student lied. She just wanted to be up near trees doing frolicy nature things and getting fit. At the back of her head there was a little voice that said "Daddy'll pay, Daddy'll pay." She knew she didn't really need the money because Dad could bail her out. Not three weeks later our heroine was back home with walking bronchitis, athlete's foot, and an allergic reaction to anything woody, wood-like, or wood-scented. And why? She didn't need the money badly enough to compensate for the physical demands of the job. Money is the ultimate young adult motivator, but sometimes even millions can't make you do a job.

But money's still a key incentive for most of us, and why shouldn't it be? Whether you're fifteen, eighteen, or twenty-two, we're all trying to move out of the reach of our parents' influence. The sooner we assume responsibilty for ourselves, the sooner we can start shedding the invisible obligations we have to our parents' values, beliefs, and expectations. No matter how much we may love and appreciate them, at some level we have to feel in some manner away or free in order to establish who we are. And that's okay too. It's totally legitimate to want to make money—to be able to go out at night, buy extra clothes or music, help out at home, or even pay for your schooling. Let's face it, money is a beautiful word—don't let anyone devalue it for you. That's the motivation to stick it out at some of the duller jobs on this planet. I filed in an office for a whole summer's worth of boredom, but by god what a bike I bought at the end of it! And I didn't have to thank anybody but myself

However, "Make money!" (with the possible exception of tree planting and other similar hard-ass jobs) is maybe not something you want to be shouting out in the middle of a job interview. Remember our environmentalist punk rock girl example? She may not have realized it, but she had a clear idea of how she wanted to earn her cash, or at least how she didn't want to earn it. Besides money, there are probably other things on your list that specify what you want, whether it be "work outdoors," "work with others my age," "work with horses," "try learning sales," or "get a job in the field of my possible career." Whether they're vague ("something athletic") or specific ("I want to sell clothes"), your goals provide the blueprint for your summer. They tell you how you're going to earn that cash. It's pretty obvious that if you want to work outdoors you'd call your provincial park, not the local mall. The closer you come to being able to exactly express what you want to do this summer, the better shot you have at actually getting the job that matches those desires.

## "I Don't Want to Brag"

Now, before you discover the 101 reasons why you're every employer's dream come true, I'll state my personal beef. Whether I'm helping students to prepare a résumé, a cover letter, or a cold call, when I encourage them to put in the specific details we've been discussing they look at me and say in a small, plaintive voice, "But I don't want to sound like I'm bragging." Hello! What are you thinking? "Maybe I'll hide all my skills and hope they'll guess. . . ."

Employers have enough applicants who can express who they are, what they've done, and how well they did a job, not to care if they never find out who you are. If you're trying to disguise your talents, hiding all the amazing things you've done—essentially holding back who you are, how do you ever expect an employer to figure you out? It's my personal belief—which I'm sure will be borne out by scientific research—that employers do not have ESP. I'm positive that they'll hire whoever seems the best qualified for the job, and that's someone confident in their abilities. Confidence—not bragging—confidence.

If it helps, I'll define the two for you. Bragging is when someone says they're "amazing and wonderful" with absolutely no proof that this is true. Braggarts give the impression that they're vastly superior to mortal human beings, and that if they're not hired the company will soon and somehow fail. Braggarts blurt out all the experience they've ever had, without focus or without listening to the employer. Braggarts put interviewers on the defensive. This is not you, and not what I'd ever suggest you do.

Confidence, on the other hand, is in the knowledge that you know who you are and what you have to contribute to any job. Employers want proof that you've done well in your previous jobs. Let me say that again. Employers now want *proof that you did well in your previous jobs,* with specific examples to that effect. Confidence is being able to clearly articulate your experience, what you have to offer, and how you can help this employer, so that the employer believes in you and wants to hire you. This is what I teach. If you don't agree with me, and you're still whimpering about bragging, take this book back to the store you got it from and start practising the phrase "Can you spare some change?" because even the people who say "Do you want fries with that?" have learned how to express themselves properly in an interview.

So with that in mind, let's begin the search for your skills so that you can find a job that's the best fit for you (and if we're feeling generous, we can throw a couple of nickels at those "ain't gonna brag" people).

## "I Have No Skills!!!!"

Despite the fact that I've suggested we search for your skills, there's no need to go on a year-long trip to Tibet to discover your inner self (unless that's one of your summer goals). You don't even have to hire a shrink, or consult a psychic. All the answers are to be found within you, and by you, with a minimum amount of work.

Let's talk about dishwashing for a minute. When my roommate Martha does the dishes, she does them with the speed and efficiency of a pit mechanic at the Indy 500. Dirt be damned, she doesn't care; when she actually does the dishes she does them all with a great flourish, stacking them every which way as if to show me and all the world "There. Look at all the dishes I did! And all in one load, I might add." When I do the dishes, on the other hand, I come at it a little more slowly and methodically. I just let the water run lightly, spray each dish with a little liquid, and scrub each one before gently putting it in "the right spot" on the dish rack. Though my roommate makes a humongous clatter in the kitchen, you'd never know I was there, except for the singing. And even after my roommate so generously does all the dishes, I sneak back in the kitchen without her knowing it, and redo about five or six of the plates and utensils that still have yucky crap on them that she missed in the blur of her dishwashing activity.

This brings me to my point, which is that a researcher discovered there are over 250 ways to wash dishes. Over 250 ways! We never think about how differently we each approach even the most simple, straightforward task of washing the kitchenware . . . but there it is. No one person will do it exactly the same way. Now imagine how many different ways there are to babysit a child, wait a table, file a report, teach baseball, and shelve a can of peas.

There are what we call "front wheel" and "back wheel" skills. Back wheel skills give the drive and front wheel skills give the direction. Everybody has the back wheel skill of dishwashing. But the ways each of us approach dishwashing make up our front wheel skills—whether it be fast, efficient, and showy, or quiet, precise, and slower. Now imagine that my roommate and I decided that we were going to get jobs dishwashing. Knowing Martha's flair for doing dishes at the speed of light, she'd be well received at a fast food place like the Sicilian Pizza Palace, which needs those dishes STAT, whatever their condition. If I worked at a place like that I'd have a breakdown running after customers' Mongo Slices, yelling "Let me just scratch off that crusty dried tomato bit underneath your plate ma'am, before you dig in!" Meanwhile, if Lady Margaret's Tea House were hiring, they'd surely appreciate the delicacy with which I approach my craft. However I just know Martha would go mental there, trying not to bang the plates.

Though we'd be trying to get what looks like the same job, *this is not the case.* We're both going to be inordinately more successful if we understand specifically how we wash our plates, and then demonstrate this knowledge to the employer who will best appreciate our talents. In this way everyone's happier—Martha, Lady Margaret, the Sicilian Pizza Palace manager, and me.

The trick in job searching is to realize that whatever task you're doing, you're most likely approaching it with your particular combination of skills, knowledge, and abilities that are uniquely different from everyone else's. If you look at employment this way, you begin to see that if someone doesn't hire you because of who you are, you probably wouldn't want to work for them anyway. Just the way I'd be miserable washing dishes at Sicilian Pizza Palace, but happy as a duchess washing dishes at the Tea House (maybe that's pushing it, but you see what I'm driving at).

So in order for you to discover your skills (front and back), you need to answer some questions for yourself. I'll guide you through a résumé counselling session, just as I do for all my clients. If it helps, have someone you trust read the questions to you, listen to your answers, and echo what you say. Sometimes hearing your experiences from another person's mouth helps you to put the pieces of the puzzle together.

## "Okay, So Maybe I Have One or Two Skills"

All right, you've been with me so far. Now I just need you to take it one step further. Every time I read these kinds of books I'm tempted to skip over the actual "write this down" part. I know you'll be tempted to do so here. Don't. If you do anything at all in this book, do the next exercise. If you don't, I can't really help you and you're lost from here on in.

I know that you're an okay person with skills to offer the summer workforce. If I were sitting with you wherever you are now I'd be able to show you this personally. In lieu of my personal appearance, all I can do is offer the same questions I've asked hundreds of students (and every single one of them has a different answer).

Give me just five minutes of your time and at the end of it you'll be well rewarded. Trust me.

## The Crucial Questions

First, write down your favourite job of all time. Then ask yourself these questions (or get someone to ask them for you). If you've never had a job use another achievement instead, such as volunteer work, something at school that you completed, or some way that you helped someone, even if it was babysitting your brother.

1. What did you do at this job?
2. What was your favourite part of the job?
3. How, exactly, did you accomplish that part of the job, i.e., if you were responsible for re-filing in an office, how did you approach it? Where did you start? How long did it take? What were the steps involved?
4. What other part of the job did you like to do? (Repeat #3.)
5. What was the hardest thing you had to do? How, specifically, did you manage to accomplish it?

6. Did you do anything at the job that no one asked you to do? (e.g., re-organize the workspace, make colourful signs for the windows)
7. How did the employers think you were doing? How do you know? (i.e., if they thought you were doing well, did they hire you back? give you a raise? tell you you were doing well?)
8. How did the customers (if any) respond to what you were doing? How did you know if it was positive?
9. Did you work with anyone else? How did that go? How, specifically, did you manage with other people?
10. If it was a stressful job, how did you cope? If it was a boring job, how did you stay awake? If it was a complicated job, how did you keep it all straight? If you had to learn to do something new in a short time, how did you manage?
11. Did anything special or out of the ordinary happen, e.g., a lifeguarding rescue at a pool, a time that you helped beyond your job description? If so, describe what happened and how you handled it.

Focus on: ***how* you did it specifically,**
**how you *know* you did it well,**
and **what was your *favourite* part of the job, or the areas that gave you the *most* satisfaction.**

## Making It All Make Sense: Looking for Themes and Patterns

As you ask these questions of each job or accomplishment, you should be looking for themes to start appearing.

Perhaps your favourite part of each job is dealing with people and helping them solve a problem. Maybe your favourite part is checking over a finished product because of your attention to detail. Maybe you like to sell things to people, or maybe what you like is pushing yourself against the clock to finish something on time. Maybe you always make people laugh while they work. Maybe you love creating an efficient workspace for yourself and others. Maybe you love working in a high-stress environment where your adrenaline is pumping all the time. Maybe the best part of your job is teaching others how to do it. Maybe you consistently come up with new ways of doing things that others adopt. Maybe you're really good at working in sync on a team to get a job done.

Start thinking about other jobs you've had, or other tasks you've done. Do any of these fit into this portrait of you? You're looking for specific things that you do, or ways of approaching your task that are consistent in most of the tasks you do, and are unique to you. See if you can make the link between one job and another, no matter how different the jobs may seem. One student I worked with was a ticket taker at a theme park ride and an assistant supervisor of horse-riding lessons. What did the two have in common? In both jobs she calmed the fears of children who were frightened. That was her input, her special talent. Once you discover how you approach a task, look for similarities in the other things you've done. I guarantee you that they'll turn up, because you bring them to every task.

It's possible that you may have combinations of things that you like to do, and are happiest if you're doing all of them together. Remember our toga party Bowl-a-Thon guy? He organized events, but his special twist was that he knew how to make the events fun for the participants. I know a student who'd been a babysitter, dog walker, and vet assistant. Her special twist? Taking the extra time to make her charges happy, whether it meant an extra hour in the park or playing a kid's favourite game over and over again. Don't forget to note your special twist.

Have you begun to get a sense of yourself now? And guess what . . . those sheets of cryptic jabberings crumpled in your hand are the beginnings of an accomplishment-based résumé. "A what?" you ask. Yep, I'm not going to show you any of those chronological, list-my-duties-and-bore-your-pants-off résumés. Remember how I mentioned future-oriented job search tools? Well you're about to develop your first, and once we clear up the scribbling and clean off the coffee stains, you'll be in business . . . literally.

CHAPTER 2

# I Need a Résumé NOW!!!

Have you been staring at a blank computer screen for the last two hours? Have you asked some friend of yours whose brother did a résumé once last summer how to "list stuff" on yours? Or would you rather punch yourself in the face, shuck corn, or watch endless reruns of bad family sitcoms rather than sit down and have to figure out a way to organize your work experience?

Often we wait and put off that résumé thing until the day before an interview, or in the frantic minutes after a phone call when someone says those frighteningly adult words "just fax it," or even that moment when we screw up the application form for the seventeenth time 'cause we can't remember the name of that stupid manager at the job two summers ago and wish like hell we'd thought to bring a résumé so that the answer to every question could be "see attached."

Résumé writing. Sheer hell. Does anyone really like doing this? I do résumés for students all the time and even I hate writing mine.

But I know there are those of you who think you've got the whole thing down pat. Congratulations! When résumé writing time rolls around you quickly write Camp Counsellor—12 weeks on a sheet of paper with your name on it, and breathe a sigh of relief. Phew! 'Cause that's it, isn't it? I mean there it is, Camp Counsellor—12 weeks, all done. Well, Camp Counsellor—12 weeks, maybe you had the thirteen-year-old girls, and instead of them bettering their minds (or at least getting to activities on time) they explored their burgeoning sexuality, deepened their tans, wrote achingly bad poetry, and ignored all orders from Camp Counsellor—12 weeks. As for you, each day was a new struggle in an effort to communicate with the little beasts. In that case, don't write a résumé, write the bestseller. 'Cause with your shorthand description, Camp Counsellor—12 weeks, we can only guess what you were up to. If you want to state only this on your résumé you can be my guest, or rather be your parents' guest all summer, cleaning out the garage. And I'm sure your parents obey minimum wage requirements. . . .

I know that you're more than Camp Counsellor—12 weeks. I know that when we write these résumés, deep down inside we're all hoping that this whole résumé writing, job hunting, nine to five experience would just go away as quickly as those four little words, Camp Counsellor—12 weeks. Sitting down to write the résumé is the first step on the road to selling ourselves, and sometimes it's an uncomfortable place to be. Take heart. Everyone has to do this little ritual at some point in their lives, and this chapter aims to make it a little easier, while encouraging you to look and sound like a person everyone would be crazy not to hire.

The current employment belief is the concept of "job fit"—where the job and the person are well matched—and that's what you'll demonstrate in your résumé and interview. Those old "responsible for" résumés focused on the tasks completed. But instead you should emphasize *how* you did the job and *what the results were*. That's what'll make your résumé special. It means being able to write down more than Camp Counsellor—12 weeks and thinking that you're done. If you put the real you on that piece of paper, like-minded employers will take notice.

## Nature Guy: A Cautionary Tale

In my last year of university I had long since given up on my ideal man; my cosmopolitan, poetry-quoting, joke-cracking, Cary Grant-sounding, suave, sophisticated king of lattés and late nights. I'd done the underground café thing, and he was clearly not going to show. Yawning my way through another party, feeling over-caffeinated and somewhat depressed, something struck me, or rather, the side of my head. The something turned out to be a Frisbee, thrown by a cute, friendly, environmentally conscious but fashion impaired party goer.

That's how I met Nature Guy. He studied lakes, sampled fish, charted nesting habits of *Harundo Rustica,* and smeared plankton on glass slides just for kicks. My old concept of Dream Man paled in comparison to this Superhero of Lakes and Streams—so earthy, so real, so *me*. Now I'm no slouch in the camping department, but it'd been a few years since I'd actually been "back to the bush." Yet when love is in the offing, there ain't no mountain high enough, or as it happened, any lake deep enough. I reached deep, and I mean deep, and got in touch with the country-fresh granola girl lurking within so that I could hang out with Nature Guy and his plankton, neglecting my much more urban temperament in my efforts to connect with this new person. Well I went ice skating, shopped at Mountain Co-op, and talked mountains and trees for a few weeks. If you'd told me in the fall that I'd go cross country skiing that winter for so long I'd get frostbite on my ear lobes, I'd have looked at you funny before taking another sip of my cappuccino and cracking another Tarantino joke with my film buddies. I took to stealing into Holt Renfrew and feeling the clothing displays, just to remind myself that DKNY still existed in the universe.

I think I realized I was in trouble when Nature Guy asked me if I wanted to go pike shooting in the spring. "Oh, what's that?" I asked in a nonchalant, I-just-forgot-momentarily voice. He enthusiastically described a trip that consisted of camping in the Vermont woods, putting on hip waders, and shooting pike with a

22-gauge shotgun. Out of my mouth I heard the words "Yeah sure, sounds like fun." I think it was at that moment that I realized all the nature fun in the world couldn't compete with an afternoon matinée and dinner at a fine restaurant.

I really wanted to be a Nature Gal but come on! I wasn't lying about liking the outdoors, but my preferred nature experience embodies the smell of grass and the crunch of fall leaves, or the soft patter of rain on the roof of a log cabin while I'm under a warm duvet; not the smoking end of a shotgun, clammy socks, and the slimy inner guts of a writhing fish.

Now you might be wondering, nature stuff aside, how was the love life? Pitiful. My exaggerations for the benefit of this guy weren't helping our relationship along at all. The truth is that he knew the whole time I wasn't as enthusiastic as I seemed, and eventually told me so. When he finally got through to me that he wasn't hiring me as a girlfriend, so to speak, I think I flipped a bit. I usually run to the dramatic, but in this case I felt that I couldn't speak to him directly; I could only walk under his window every night to see the light on in his room and make sure he was still alive . . . coupled with watching a lot of movies, talking to all my friends about it, and crying under the moon. When I finally came to and got back to my life, I would have felt completely idiotic about the whole thing except that, scarily enough, most of my friends have had similar experiences.

Moral of the story: know who you are, know what you want, and co-ordinate the two. Whether it's your love life or your résumé, you'll only make it easier on yourself. Welcome to sanity.

## This Is Not a Format Book

I know it'd be a hell of a lot easier if I gave you a diagram and a couple of charts to show you this whole résumé thing. You could copy it out and we could call it a day. I've struggled with this chapter *forever* because I was trying to find a way to do that for you. The truth is, folks, the way that these more contemporary and fresher résumés are being written doesn't take too well to formatting. The difference between "make a list" and accomplishment-based résumés is that with the latter no one on this planet can have the same résumé as you. Telling you one way to do your résumé is kind of like me telling you the perfect one-liner to use on the babes . . . virtually impossible, because no one line works for all people in all situations. That's part of the beauty of these résumés—they're uniquely designed to show *your* experience and your skills, as well as the jobs you've had. If you called me up we could go for coffee and chat about the greatness that you are, but since you're so comfy on your couch, let's just see if we can do this phone call-free.

## "But My Experience Is Pretty Much Like Everyone Else's"

Here's an entry from an acceptable résumé:

*Lifeguard —Happy Pool People Company—Summer 1989*

- *responsible for care and maintenance of apartment pool*
- *responsible for safety of all people in pool and on deck*
- *responsible for summer lifeguard rotation schedule*

This screams BORING to me and every employer who reads it. It's from an old résumé of mine, and you guessed it, my phone wasn't ringing off the hook. It tells me jack about how I guarded the pool, how I felt about it, and whether I kept the pool running at all. Maybe a record 400 people drowned. Maybe everybody *but* the two-year-olds peed in the pool. Maybe my poolside nickname was Goober because of all the times I spat on the deck. Sure I was responsible, that was in the contract when I was hired—but did I do it? I can't expect a a blue ribbon for doing my job description. Big whoopy thrill. That's what my pay cheque was for, or else I would've been fired. Employers have too many résumés like this sitting on their desks to start assuming my super stardom. I have to tell them something they want to know.

Now compare the above to the following summations as completed by actual students:

*Lifeguard—Summer 199-*

- *My greatest accomplishment all summer was teaching a young girl to swim in the deep end so that she could play with her friends.*
- *While most lifeguards never see a rescue situation, in one summer I performed three successful rescues on non-swimmers who became tired and panicked.*
- *Though I enjoy guarding immensely and talking to the people who frequent the pool, my greatest satisfaction this past summer came from joining a lifeguarding team that competed all over the province. We were the only all-female guard team to make it into the National Finals.*

- *The very busy pool I managed had a notoriously bad filter system that broke down with whimsical regularity, often forcing us to close the pool. Within a week or two I learned the tricks to fix it quickly, and soon even the pool supervisors would call for me because I was the only one who could keep the pool up and running.*

Each of these examples, whether short or long, says volumes about each of the people who wrote them down. They sound great, and yet none of them saved 200 orphans from a fire, or made a million dollars. They're regular people like you, and from these excerpts alone I feel that I both know and like them. Now at some point when they sat down to write their résumés, each of these students was a "Lifeguard—12 weeks." From an employer's point of view, maybe "anyone" could do the job. And they'll hire "anyone" unless you step in there and introduce yourself. Why compete with "anyone" when there's no competition for being you? The difference between these examples and the one before is striking in the amount of *personality* that shines through. And personality is what many, many résumés lack. Why is this important? Because employers will want to know more about who you are. You also demonstrate proof that you can do a job well, which furthers their confidence that the résumé isn't a pack of lies.

Now this is not to suggest that you pull out your tea set and your pipe to recount book-length anecdotes of your days on the job (*"On Day Seven, little Jimmy came running to me with snot on his face and said, "Baba weewee," which meant, as I had come to understand, "I trust you Sally to wipe my nose clean"*). A résumé is still a precise and sharp *summation* of what you've done. All I'm suggesting is that since employers are likely to know the job description, why not offer them some more beneficial information in the short space you have?

## "If I'm So Special, Why Am I Still Having Trouble Writing a Résumé?"

I thought it might help you if you could relate this résumé process to someone else who doesn't think they're special, a student with only so much experience who needs a job this summer. I want to introduce you to Steve. Steve's a great guy. His friends like him, his parents have no complaints (no more than the usual take-out-the-trash-turn-down-the-music-stop-dressing-up-the-dog ones anyway), and he has that kind of potential in him that convinces you he'll have a great career being . . . *something*. Some day. Steve's not a hundred percent sure on that career part. At this point he'd like to be either a Vice President Marketing meistro at some major company, or a television newscaster. That's not important right now. He may well do both. Steve wants a job this summer, which, I'm sure you'd agree, is a fairly legitimate request. Steve's problem is this: his job experience up to this point has involved only dishes, and their process from dirty to clean. That's right, Steve is the dishwashing king. Every paid work experience he's had involved china, porcelain, or silverware, and the guy is so sick of dishes that he eats off paper plates. This summer all Steve wants is a job without Palmolive in the job description.

Steve is concerned. He knows he wants SOME job, and he knows he has SOME skills. But he's not sure of either, and all those "skills" seem to point right back to the dishwashing milieu. Problem. Steve is terrified of becoming old and grey and never leaving the steam-filled, dirty-dish hell of the diner he's been working at part-time this year. He's thinking he might like to try the big bucks, cut-throat world of business, something he passed on after a week of filing a year ago at his uncle's law practice. At that time he was more interested in the social scene as camp dishwashing assistant than wearing a tie, so he ditched the office job his uncle got him. A summer of suds and sun suited him fine. When the dishwashing job at a local diner came up it seemed like a natural jump. But what was a good idea and some extra spending money at the time now has Steve feeling trapped into having "dishwashing experience only." Plagued by nightly dreams of lipstick stains and crusty leftovers, this summer he wants back into the heady world of office work (suits, ties, and the only water for miles safely stored in water coolers with little paper cups). But he doesn't want to have to ask his uncle now, having burned his employment bridges with a blowtorch the last time out.

How can Steve get into business when his job experiences—minus the job he bailed on—all point to dishwashing? Let's see what Steve, having wisely come to me for help, is going to do about his résumé.

Steve Santerini
4852 Av. du Parc
Montreal, PQ

(514) 279-4754

Work Experience

office clerk - responsible for filing

Camp Hooligan - dishwasher

- responsible for dishes

Norm's Diner, dishwasher, busboy

Extracurricular/Special skills

hockey

rugby

soccer

basketball

food drive

references: on request

Steve has succumbed to Résumé Writer Panic Syndrome. Symptoms include writing everything down really fast and really small so that maybe people won't read it and just hire you because . . . you can spell. The cure for this terrible affliction, from which almost all of us suffer, is coming in the next several pages. So Steve, we'll consider this your first draft, a sort of gathering of ideas. We've got to use those dishwashing days to their best advantage. My advice to Steve is SAY SOMETHING about what he's been doing with all those dishes.

## 1. Say Something

Although Steve's résumé covers the obvious, it's merely a list and nothing more. It neither displays Steve's talents through the content, nor jazzes up the reading of it through style. Let's work on the the content half first. As I've previously discussed, saying you've been there doesn't tell the employer a whole hell of a lot.

I can see that he probably did something in his job as dishwasher, and I'm pretty sure he was responsible for it, but I'm not sure he actually did it. I want to know what Steve was actually doing. Another employer may not even take the time to realize that there are actually three jobs on Steve's résumé. Did *you* realize there were three jobs on his résumé?

Once you've made the requisite list of things that you did, it's time to go back to those questions you answered in Chapter 1 and find out what gave you satisfaction in the job you did. Remember the essential question, "How exactly did you do the job?" Find the proof, or the specific examples that show your claims are true.

Steve is a thoughtful guy, and he listens carefully to what I say before trying it himself. On the right is an excerpt from the five pages Steve handed to me.

> Norm's Diner - Busboy
> The responsibilities included in the daily maintenance of a busy diner dishwashing area are duties such as sorting all the essential dishware and utensils, creating efficient loads of racks of dishes, making sure that the ready dishes are in appropriate and accessible places to be retrieved by wait staff, supervising all the machines, and managing the details of organizing the many varieties of dishes and glasses. The responsibilities also include maintaining the clean tubs for sets of dirty dishes and making sure that tables are cleared on a regular basis. This requires a patient and practical person who can oversee all aspects of this job, as well as be responsible for getting dishes clean and readied for the restaurant patrons.

This is a fine description of what a dishwasher does. What I want to know is, what did *Steve* do as a dishwasher? I can't find Steve anywhere in this description. And what does "overseeing all aspects of this job" mean anyway? I picture Steve with binoculars sitting in an easy chair in the corner, occasionally checking up on the dishes' behaviour. I want to hear Steve's voice. I want to know what Steve liked doing. I want Steve to look and sound amazing. . . .

## 2. Make Every Word Count

Steve's second draft can be summed up in four little words: "I was a dishwasher." Why? Even if you read the whole thing through (and you get extra bonus points for following this book so closely), you're one out of about three people who would—and none of them is an employer. If you don't put yourself in the job description, employers won't either.

Making every word count means that every word has a purpose in the sentence. In the nineties style résumé we're going for here, it also means that the word "I" can be involved, so we know that it was YOU who was there working and being practical, patient, etc., etc.

Go through the Chapter 1 questions again, and the notes you took. Look for the examples that will give you the proof you need to transform a general statement about what the job entailed into a specific description of you at work. (Flip to the skills list at the end of this book for ideas on particular terms you might use.)

Steve's trying so hard to give me what I want, but he's understandably confused. His biggest fear—that the only job he can do in the world is wash dishes—is blocking his ability to see all the generalized skills that he performed every weekend in the dishroom, and in all other aspects of his regular student life. All Steve needs to do is take a deep breath and think about what he was actually doing at the diner. I wanted to know too, so I asked.

**So tell me what you do at the diner.**
I'm a dishwasher. But first I was a busboy.

**Tell me about that.**
Oh, being a busboy? That was a breeze. I walked around with a plastic tub, collected dirty dishes after people left, and dumped the dishes in the tubs. I was only on during the real weekend rushes. It paid crap but it was pretty basic. I only did it for two or three weeks.

**What happened then?**
Their weekend dishwasher quit. I convinced them that since I did dishes at camp I could be their dishwasher. It was a more than double pay hike. I wasn't even getting minimum before that.

**So you moved up. How was that?**

Restaurants are a little different from camps. At camp the dishes were always clean from the meal before. They got dirty once. They were cleaned once. In a restaurant, the dishes are never done. People tend to keep coming in and wanting to be served. It makes for endless dirty dishes.

**Sounds stressful. How did you manage?**

Not so hot. I mean I sucked big time. I'd get six loads of plates through the dishwasher and after half an hour I'd start to relax. But then I'd notice these stressed waiters coming into the dishroom. They'd look at me, then at the dishes, then they'd look at me again, and then they'd leave.

**What did you do?**

I finally asked what was wrong. Turns out they were looking for cutlery. With dishes you've gotta rotate things around so everything gets clean at about the same time, or else you've got hundreds of clean plates but nothing to eat with. Even toast requires a utensil.

**So you had to anticipate the wait staff's needs.**

Yeah, exactly. Like another thing. To save time I used to cram all the cutlery together—knives, spoons, whatever—and just shove them into the cutlery trays. Then I realized that that made it harder for the wait staff because they'd be picking the forks from the spoons. In a rush, you don't want to be doing that.

**So you found a way of making the system more efficient for others.**

Uh huh. I had to do extra sorting at the beginning of the cycle, but the staff liked me a lot. They kinda hated the guy before me because he used to put in a load, go for a smoke, and socialize with the manager or something. I realized pretty soon after taking the job that for a good dishwasher, the job is never done. It's chaos.

**The dishroom was organized after that.**

Yeah, I got into a good rhythm. Not that it wasn't messy back there or anything. But that's usually a good sign because it means you're always taking in more dirty dishes and not leaving them out front to rot in the soaking bins. But after a while I had to talk to the wait staff.

**Tell me about that.**

Well, they were rushed into doing things like stuffing their tables' napkins and garbage into the glasses, or chucking different plates and cups and saucers and bowls and platters all into the dish bins along with ashtrays and crayons and lasagna. Back in the dishroom I've gotta deal with all this stuff. It's not just that it's a mess, or that I have to spend so much time ditching the garbage, or that I was breaking plateware left, right and centre, but that I was making twice the trips to get the bus pans.

**What did you do about it?**

Well, I asked them to stop doing it.

**How did you ask them? And how did they take it?**

They grumbled about it. But I kinda showed them the advantages. Like, if they did thirty seconds more work on the front end, they got their dishes way faster. I even had some extra time to bring racks of essental pop and water glasses and stuff to the front counter, which they all really appreciated during the rushes.

**So you presented them with a win/win deal, created more of a team atmosphere at the restaurant, and basically made the diner work more efficiently, saving both time, customer complaints, and money from fewer broken glasses.**

Yes. I guess you're right. The diner owner really wants me there full time this summer. It's good money and I'm tempted, but I need a life. I'm really proud of what I do but I don't think a career in dishwashing is my calling.

**Now we have something to work with.**

We do?

So off I went to make notes on Steve's amazing examples of proof to incorporate into his résumé before he writes his next draft.

**Dishwasher Job—Norm's Diner**

Things that Show Growth in the Job

1. First he was a busboy, then he was promoted to dishwasher.
2. First no one talked to him, then everyone loved him.
3. First he was a slave to a badly organized system, then he re-organized and streamlined it so that he was the master of a successful strategy.
4. First he was mute, then he communicated his needs.
5. First he just aimed to fulfill the job requirements, then he took initiative to do extras, like bringing out needed racks and re-organizing the system.

How Does Steve Know He's Amazing?

1. The job gets done.
   But even more concrete, the feedback is:
2. Staff love having him on their shift.
3. The owner wants him full time this summer.
4. Co-workers note a positive difference in the way the job gets done.

**Skills to Highlight**

Ability to communicate and work as part of a team, organizational skills, anticipation of others' needs, ability to prioritize important tasks.

Steve is staring at the notes I made of his experiences. I can tell he's never thought of his job this way before. He asks me what the theory behind this is and I tell him that it's found in the next crucial step in résumé writing.

## 3. Show Proof

This is one of the trickier concepts behind résumés, cover letters, and interviews. You may not get it perfect right away, but I know you can handle it. This is how it goes: you're not only trying to show your potential employer that you did the job, but you're also going to prove that you did the job well. Often proof can be demonstrated through movement; that is, an increase in responsibility or knowledge during the period you worked at the job.

I can hear you shouting, "Karen, stop the madness!" I know, I know, and Steve is feeling that way too. But if you look over the notes I've taken you'll probably see where the proof is. Steve didn't just wash dishes; he organized the system, made it efficient, communicated with his co-workers to find out what they needed and then what he needed to do the job well, and as a result the staff love him and he's saving them time and customer complaints. And here Steve was thinking that he was just washing dishes. If we look for the same skills in his other work and activities, I'll bet we'll find them.

"But they're gonna think I'm a big cheese meister!" Steve protests. Yet showing proof is actually the fastest, easiest, and most understandable way around the problem of how not to brag. Let your work do the talking for you. It isn't Steve saying, "I'm the best dishwasher in the world, ha, HA, HAA. Fear me earthlings." He can let us know how well he did by simply telling us the facts and their results.

I now tell Steve to go back to his computer, envision his dishwashing legacy, and let the words flow through his dishpan hands. Steve informed me that his hands were still silky soft, thank you very much, and ready to type out his masterpiece. When I read it, I had to agree.

Steve Santerini
4852 Av. du Parc
Montreal, PQ
(514) 279-4754

Work Experience
office clerk - responsible for filing
Camp Big Hawk - dishwasher
- responsible for dishes
Dishwasher - Norm's Diner
I started at this busy diner as a busboy, but within two weeks I was promoted to dishwashing. Clean dishes are essential to a restaurant's business. I created an organized, efficient system, where I:
1) prioritize the different loads of dishware, glasses, and cutlery so that all items are available at all times,
2) anticipate the needs of the wait staff by doing tasks such as separating cutlery for faster retrieval and bringing clean essentials to the front during busy hours, and
3) consistently keep my end running smoothly by bringing in bus pans before they become over-filled.

As a result of my re-organization, I've saved everyone time and made all of our jobs easier. My co-workers have experienced less stress on the job, and have asked to be scheduled on the same shifts so that we can continue to work as a cohesive team. The owner of the diner has asked me to stay on full time this summer.

Extracurricular
hockey
rugby
soccer
basketball
food drive

Special Skills
- computer skills
references: on request

Hey, not bad Steve! The content of your résumé is really shaping up. For our next trick, we've got to make some sense of the overall mess of a résumé we started with.

## 4. From Chaos Comes Meaning (with a Little Organization)

Despite Steve's natural inclination to include everything he's ever done, now that some of that vast white space is disappearing all that information isn't so necessary. Let's figure out what stays and what goes.

**a) Eliminate the undesirables.**
Steve's one-week stint as an office clerk isn't going to do him any favours. If the job lasted only a week he might want to include it briefly at the end. But since he quit, he's better to ditch it.

**b) Toss out the notion of steadfast chronological order.**
Create your order based on what's most important for the employer to see. Put that first. If any jobs get repetitive (i.e., six jobs as a cashier), explain the most recent, your favourite, and/or the one with the reference. The others you can list at the end. Or leave them off all together if it's too crowded.

**c) Fight the urge to list all your "interests" or hobbies.**
Really, who needs to know whether or not you play a million sports or love animals? *Unless it relates to the job in some way.* For instance, a veterinary clinic would want to know you love animals. A commitment to one or two sports shows discipline and dedication. Playing the piano, learning a language, being a debater, fixing a car, the same. Just don't overload the reader with your leisure activities, unless you're low on work experience and you're using them to demonstrate skills. If Steve wants to work in an office, putting in his computer skills makes sense.

**d) If you've got room, separate Volunteer Work out from the crowd.**
This section can often count as work experience (see Part 3). Don't bury it at the bottom of the résumé, especially if the skills are applicable to the job.

**e) Education isn't everything.**
Including your education is important, but putting it first slows down the reading of your résumé. (But, again, if the education is relevant to the job, of course you can put it first.)

I send Steve off to polish up the content of his CV, and Steve has been paying attention, because he returns with a strong looking and sounding résumé.

Steve Santerini
4852 Av. du Parc
Montreal, PQ
(514) 279-4754

Work Experience

Dishwasher - Norm's Diner - Sept. 1996 to present

I started at this busy diner as a busboy, but within two weeks I was promoted to dishwashing, solely my responsibility. Clean dishes are essential to a restaurant's business. I created an organized, efficient system, where I:

1) prioritize the different loads of dishware, glasses, and cutlery, so that all items are available at all times,

2) anticipate the needs of the wait staff by doing tasks such as separating cutlery for faster retrieval, bringing clean essentials to the front during busy hours, and

3) consistently keep my end running smoothly by bringing in bus pans before they became over-filled.

As a result of my re-organization, I've saved everyone time and made all of our jobs easier. My co-workers have experienced less stress on the job, and have asked to be scheduled on the same shifts so that we can continue to work as a cohesive team. The owner of the diner has asked me to stay on full time this summer.

Dishwasher - Camp Big Hawk - Summer 1996

Myself and a co-worker washed 250 camper and staff dishes, 3 meals a day, 6 days a week, for 7 weeks. Although the only job requirement was to thoroughly clean all the dishes (and accompanying pots, pans, and cooking trays) by the next meal, we consistently completed our work swiftly and ahead of schedule. This efficiency was achieved due to creating a familiar routine, dividing our tasks to match our personal specialties, and coordinating our efforts to keep the pace continuous and quick.

Volunteer Work

Daily Bread Bank - Committe Head - During the school year, I motivated my class to collect food for monthly food drives, through announcements, pledges, and contests. Over an 8-month period, our class sent at least 4 full cardboard boxes of food each month to a nonprofit Food Bank.

Extracurricular

Hockey - From age 13 to the present I've played hockey four or more days a week, consisting of 3 days of practice and 2 or 3 games. I now play in the Junior B League. I enjoy hockey for its teamwork, strategy, and the good feeling that comes from playing an exceptional game.

also on school baseball team (spring), soccer team (fall)

Currently Attending: Philip Joseph High School, completed Grade 11.

Computer Skills: Data Processing; Macentosh Word, ClarisWorks, Windows '95

references: on request

Great work! Steve is coming across as a well-rounded, motivated, and exceptional candidate. Most importantly, he comes across as a person rather than as a few lines on a page. The next step is to get people to read this masterpiece. For that, we need Style . . . .

## 5. Make It Look Sharp

Now let's cover some of the ways that Steve can make his résumé and its strong content stand out. Résumés are 50 percent content and 50 percent style. But style is maybe a little more important, because all the great writing in the world won't be read if it's presented as something you'd use to scoop cat litter with.

**a) Make it catch the eye.**
Your goal is to make the employer want to run his or her eye down the page.

**b) Organize the material into sections.**
Typically you want to list first your work experience that relates to the job you're applying for, then if you have other jobs that don't apply, just list them under Additional Work Experience.

Don't be too concerned about chronological order. Put first the most important job that most fits the job you're applying for, or that demonstrates your best skills. Let the dates speak for themselves.

Other categories are things like Education, Birthdate, Volunteer Work, Extracurricular Activities, and Related Skills. Make up your own headings according to the experience you want to demonstrate.

**c) Make your name big.**
The key item on the résumé is your name. That's who they'll be calling up for the interview. Don't be afraid to put it front and centre. You want them to be thinking your name as they read about your experience.

**d) Use bolds or different font sizes to draw attention to job titles and sections.**
To help the eye skim the page, you can highlight what you want employers to read.

Steve listened closely again and seemed relieved. This he understands. He came back with this résumé:

## Steve Santerini

4852 Av. du Parc,
Montreal, PQ
**(514) 279-4754**

### Work Experience-

**DISHWASHER - Norm's Diner** *Sept. 1996 to present*

I started at this busy diner as a busboy, but within two weeks I was promoted to dishwashing, solely my responsibility. Clean dishes are essential to a restaurant's business. I created an organized, efficient system, where I:

**1** *prioritize the different loads of dishware, glasses, and cutlery, so that all items are available at all times,*

**2** *anticipate the needs of the wait staff by doing tasks such as separating cutlery for faster retrieval, bringing clean essentials to the front during busy hours, and*

**3** *consistently keep my end running smoothly by bringing in bus pans before they became overfilled.*

As a result of my re-organization, I've saved everyone time and made all of our jobs easier. My coworkers have experienced less stress on the job, and have asked to be scheduled on the same shifts so that we can continue to work as a cohesive team. The owner of the diner has asked me to stay on full time this summer.

**DISHWASHER - Camp Big Hawk** - *Summer 1996*

Myself and a co-worker washed 250 camper and staff dishes, 3 meals a day, 6 days a week, for 7 weeks. Though the only job requirement was to thoroughly clean all the dishes (and accompanying pots, pans, and cooking trays) by the next meal, we consistently completed our work swiftly and ahead of schedule.This efficiency was achieved due to creating a familiar routine, dividing our tasks to match our personal specialties, and coordinating our efforts to keep the pace continuous and quick.

### Volunteer Work

**DAILY BREAD BANK - Committe Head** - During the school year I motivated my class to collect food for monthly food drives, through announcements, pledges, and contests. Over an 8-month period, our class sent at least 4 full cardboard boxes of food each month to a non-profit Food Bank.

**Extracurricular**

Hockey - From age 13 to the present I've played hockey 4 or more days a week, consisting of 3 days of practice and 2 or 3 games.I now play in the Junior B League.I enjoy hockey for its teamwork, strategy, and the good feeling that comes from playing an exceptional game.
also on school baseball team (spring), soccer team (fall)

Currently Attending: Philip Joseph High School, completed Grade 11.

**Computer Skills:** Data Processing; Macentosh Word, ClarisWorks, Windows '95

*references*: on request

Whoa, Steve! Stop that style train buddy . . . remember that résumé rule of thumb:

## 6. KISS, or "Keep It Simple Steve"

In simplicity there's style. Going overboard makes your résumé an unreadable eyesore.

**a) Keep the whole résumé in the same font.**
"Font" is the style of lettering and it should be preferably a plain one (e.g. Chicago, Palatino, or Times), because the print will hurt the reader's eyes if it's all over the place or is too cramped or fancy.

**b) Spread it out.**
The key to an appealing looking résumé is actually the white space between the entries. The white space is like a little eye breather, and highlights the well-written words in their own island of space on the page. You're now the publisher of your own life, so start thinking in terms of layout and design. For instance, if you're working on a computer, bullets [•] look way more clean and professional than those puny hyphens [-]. And where you do use hyphens, try a full dash instead (shift-option-dash on a Mac computer) for a full-bodied effect [—].

**c) Consistency, consistency, consistency.**
If you do it once, do it the same throughout that section. So if the date is in the left column for the first job, it should be in the left column all the way down. If you capitalize your job title in the first description, do it that way throughout the résumé. Even the spacing should be as consistent as possible. If you leave one space between each heading in the first description, carry it through the résumé. You may have to play around with different set-ups to get it all in and even. Change things around if you feel strongly about what should be highlighted. For example, one Human Resources manager suggested that you might want to put the job title first, in order to emphasize the person doing the job rather than the company. It depends on your personal taste—and you get to choose.

**d) Save the bolds and larger type sizes for the important things.**
Bold your name, your address, the places you've worked, and the section headings. If you want to draw attention to something else that's key for the job, bold it. But otherwise, use the fancy stuff sparingly to draw the eye to each section of print. If you think there's too much bold on the page, another option to consider is "small caps" (Dishwasher—NORM'S DINER).

I sent Steve back to his computer to complete his final draft.

# Steve Santerini

4852 Av. du Parc
Montreal, PQ
**(514) 279-4754**

## Work Experieince

**Dishwasher—Norm's Diner**
September 1996 -present
I started at this busy diner as a busboy, but within two weeks I was promoted to dishwashing, solely my responsibility. Clean dishes are essential to a restaurant's business. I created an organized, efficient system, where I:
1) prioritize the different loads of dishware, glasses, and cutlery, so that all items are available at all times,
2) anticipate the needs of the wait staff by doing tasks such as separating cutlery for faster retrieval, bringing clean essentials to the front during busy hours, and
3) consistently keep my end running smoothly by bringing in bus pans before they became over-filled.
As a result of my re-organization, I've saved everyone time and made all of our jobs easier. My co-workers have experienced less stress on the job, and have asked to be scheduled on the same shifts, so that we can continue to work as a cohesive team. The owner of the diner has asked me to stay on full time this summer.

**Camp Big Hawk - dishwasher**
**summer '96**
Myself and a co-worker washed 250 camper and staff dishes, 3 meals a day, 6 days a week, for 7 weeks. Though the only job requirement was to thoroughly clean all the dishes (and accompanying pots, pans, and cooking trays) by the next meal, we consistently completed our work swiftly and ahead of schedule. This efficiency was achieved due to creating a familiar routine, dividing our tasks to match our personal specialties, and coordinating our efforts to keep the pace continuous and quick.

## Volunteer Work

**Daily Bread Bank - Committe Head** During the school year, I motivated my class to collect food for monthly food drives, through announcements, pledges, and contests. Over an 8-month period, our class sent at least 4 full cardboard boxes of food each month to a non-profit Food Bank.

## Extracurricular

• **Hockey** - From age 13 to the present I've played hockey 4 or more days a week, consisting of 3 days of practise and 2 or 3 games. I now play in the Junior B League. I enjoy hockey for its team-work, strategy, and the good feeling that comes from playing an exceptional game.
• 1st string school baseball team (spring)
• 2nd string soccer team (fall).

**Computer Skills** - Data Processing; Macentosh Word, ClarisWorks, Windows '95

**Attending:** Philip Joseph High School, completed Grade 11

***References Available Upon Request***

Steve is so almost there it isn't funny. He's got the white space happening, the simplicity of style, the great content of his job descriptions. He wants to send out this sucker now and be done with it, but I send him back one last time to double check the small details. Steve, tiring of my résumé games, might have been more upset—but as in dishwashing, he knows the job is never done.

## 7. Details, Details, Details

This is the last stop you have to make before you can call your résumé complete. Run that baby through spell check, or haul out your dictionary. CVs can be made or murdered by the littlest thing, especially in jobs that require a keen attention to detail. Also, employers are always looking for reasons to oust a résumé from the stack on their desk. Don't give them any reason to do so with yours.

Double check:

- spelling
- dates
- addresses, and even more important, phone numbers
- consistency of style
- font sizes

Fine-tune the writing if necessary, and make sure that you've included all the essential information you want employers to know. When I write résumés for people I have at least one, if not two other people read it over, after both the draft and at this final stage. After staring at the screen or the page for a while, it's amazing what you can miss, especially when it's your own experience and you're overly familiar with it. I highly recommend that you let another pair of eyes view your résumé before you send it out.

The work's been done and the verdict is in . . . Steve is more than just a dishwasher. Sure his experience is limited at this point, but his potential isn't. All of Steve's skills are ready to be discovered by a lucky employer. And I'm going to suggest a perfect use for those very skills, after Steve is done correcting this sucker.

# Steve Santerini

4852 Av. du Parc
Montreal, PQ H2V 4E6
**(514) 279-4745**

## Work Experience

**Norm's Diner—Dishwasher**
**September 1996 - present**

I started at this busy diner as a busboy, but within two weeks I was promoted to dishwashing, solely my responsibility. Clean dishes are essential to a restaurant's business. I created an organized, efficient system, where I:
1) prioritize the different loads of dishware, glasses, and cutlery, so that all items are available at all times,
2) anticipate the needs of the wait staff by doing tasks such as separating cutlery for faster retrieval, bringing clean essentials to the front during busy hours, and
3) consistently keep my end running smoothly by bringing in bus pans before they became over-filled.

As a result of my re-organization, I've saved everyone time and made all of our jobs easier. My co-workers have experienced less stress on the job, and have asked to be scheduled on the same shifts so that we can continue to work as a cohesive team. The owner of the diner has asked me to stay on full time this summer.

**Camp Big Hawk—Dishwasher**
**Summer 1996**

Myself and a co-worker washed 250 camper and staff dishes, 3 meals a day, 6 days a week, for 7 weeks. Though the only job requirement was to thoroughly clean all the dishes (and accompanying pots, pans, and cooking trays) by the next meal, we consistently completed our work swiftly and ahead of schedule. This efficiency was achieved due to creating a familiar routine, dividing our tasks to match our personal specialties, and coordinating our efforts to keep the pace continuous and quick.

## Volunteer Work

**Daily Bread Bank—Committee Head** During the school year I motivated my class to collect food for monthly food drives, through announcements, pledges, and contests. Over an 8-month period, our class sent at least 4 full large cardboard boxes of food each month to a non-profit Food Bank.

## Extracurricular

• Hockey—From age 13 to the present I've played hockey 4 or more days a week, consisting of 3 days of practice and 2 or 3 games. I now play in the Junior B League. I enjoy hockey for its teamwork, strategy, and the good feeling that comes from playing an exceptional game.
• 1st string school baseball team (spring)
• 2nd string soccer team (fall)

**Attending**—Philip Joseph High School, completed Grade 11

**Computer Skills**—Data Processing; Microsoft Word, ClarisWorks, Windows '95

***References Available Upon Request***

Steve is now in possession of a wicked base résumé. He can expand from here into focusing this résumé for any specific job or application he wants to pursue, within reason of course.

## 8. Made to Order

In order to focus your résumé for a particular job or company, the key is to search in your experience for the most applicable jobs or parts of jobs, and then highlight those in the résumé. Do this by:

**a) Changing the order.**

Moving your maintenance experience to the forefront when trying for a construction job is probably better than putting the waiting job first. Leave chronological order by the wayside and let your experience do the talking.

**b) Expanding on the applicable parts.**

Take the time to explain more about the things that apply. For instance, one of the students I saw wanted to get a job either waiting tables or working at a record store. She had worked in a café that was also a record store, so in her record store résumé we highlighted all the extra work she'd done helping out the record store staff when her counter service got slow, and emphasized her general knowledge of how a music store is run. In her waitressing résumé we kept the extra help in the store to one line, and concentrated on all the work she did in the café.

**c) Highlighting the skills needed in the job you're aiming for.**

Even if your experience isn't directly applicable, think about what skills you'd need and then accentuate them in your job description. For example, a waiter has to work well under pressure, so you could give an example of how you managed a stressful job. Or a construction job requires consistent, hard physical effort, so underscore the hard work you did scraping and cleaning a boat, or tree planting.

# This Is Way Too Wacky for Me!

Some students who are applying to very conservative office jobs are reluctant to use the content format I've demonstrated, and I think that's more than okay. You're the one who has to feel comfortable with what you're presenting. You may just be a "list it" kind of person. This is not a test. I won't get mad at you if you want to do it the old way. Just remember that many, many of my students have found great success with these résumés. And even if you choose a point-form approach, you can still say something particular about the way you did the job or how you grew in it.

## This Thing Isn't Wacky Enough for the Real Me!

If you feel that your true expression is even more creative, by all means go for it. I've come across many students who've made headway by being ultra funny or creative with their résumés. One student told me a story involving her dad's toy company. He often receives résumés directly, but always passes them down to Human Resources without looking at them. What stopped his eye? An applicant had done up his résumé like a game board, with the object of the game being to hire him. It was cleverly done, and our toy company owner looked at it, laughed, then picked up the phone and called the guy to invite him in for an interview. Whoever he was, this person took a risk.

On the other hand, sometimes if your creativity is rejected you'll know you're not going to like the job. One student I know is a great waitress and a very creative artist. In order to apply for a job at a restaurant where she thought she'd like to work, she created a filo hamburger, with each layer (lettuce, cheese, tomato) making up a piece of her cover letter. She proudly took this work of art and humour into the restaurant, where the manager barely glanced at it and told her to leave her résumé and call back the next week. She was hurt until I pointed out that she probably wouldn't have liked working there. Brightening up right away, she agreed wholeheartedly and got a job at another restaurant within the week. They loved her hamburger. She loves her job.

Sometimes the wackiness is in the writing. One enthusiastic student has a résumé that talks of her "amassing unheard-of tips" and describes a boss she worked with as "slurpee-slurping and oversexed." Crazy? She has an excellent waitressing job as a result of that résumé; as well, theatre companies have hired her on her résumé and cover letter alone. Half of it is in the clever writing, and I think the other half is in the confidence she had to put herself on the page. Her résumé might backfire in a more conservative setting, but then this student would never want to work there.

## The One- or Two-Page Debate

If you're under nineteen the rule of thumb is one page only, since you most likely don't have enough relevant experience to justify two pages. This isn't a bad thing, because a one-page limit will get you to edit your résumé sharply so that only the most relevant information appears. Employers rarely get on to the second page anyway. And there's nothing so unappealing as a résumé that trails off in the top third of the second page. Some of you start to add things to make it look more substantial, and then the whole thing's a mess. Don't go there. Edit yourself, and you'll come across more professionally.

For those of you with more job experience, I still think that a one-page résumé is ample for most situations. If you do go to two pages, make sure that *the most relevant* information is on page one. You'd be surprised at how many people put their actual work experience on the second page, after they've listed all their education from kindergarden onwards (not necessary) and all the awards they've ever won for activities that have nothing to do with the job they're applying for.

## A Brief Summary of This Whole Chapter

The moral of the story, folks, is be true to you. Trust me and your own experience, and create the résumé that suits it.

As for Steve? I figured out the perfect way he could use his dishwashing skills to break into business: working in an office mailroom. It's a good entry-level job that he won't be too young for. The same principle of sorting and organizing is in play. And he'll get a good idea of what other departments do, which will help him to focus his general enthusiasm for business. Finally, while he picks up and delivers the mail he can start using more of those people skills to make some friends in different offices—and set himself up for an even better job at eighteen.

But before Steve can do that, he's got to write a cover letter. You know, that other little piece of paper that sits on top of the résumé when you slip it in the envelope.

Never heard of it? I've got you covered. Check the next chapter.

CHAPTER 3

# Cover Me, I'm Going In

Now you may be wondering, "If my cover letter goes on top of my résumé, why am I doing it second?" The answer is that the cover letter is the icing on the cake, the *pièce de résistance,* the guest star rather than the supporting cast. It is, in short, the most "out there" tool in the job application package. This is where you go *mano e mano* (that's Latin) with a blank page, upon which you're expected to create some kind of meaningful message to a faceless reader. You won't always need a cover letter for every job you're applying for, but they're becoming more and more important in selling yourself to employers.

I'm going to make a confession to you. I put off writing this chapter until the last possible second, and I'll tell you why. I hate writing cover letters. I'm always tempted to hide behind professional-sounding phrases rather than write something that exposes the real me. And since I (the supposed "writer") was having that feeling, I worried about how to tell you, the reader (perhaps more given to an analytical, scientific, or straightforward approach to life) to take risks in writing your cover letter.

I resolved my inner conflict by determining this: you, at home, have the ultimate responsibility for how you're going to get yourself employed. It's your choice. I'll tell you about the way I see cover letters being written for positive effect, especially in situations where the addressee has no clue who you are. You decide how far you want to take it.

So pour yourself another piping hot beverage of preference, wipe the sweat off your résumé-wrinkled brow, and let's start this sucker by expanding on what you already know.

## The Cover Letter Speaks!

The résumé that you've just completed (well done, by the way) forms the backbone of your self-presentation. In broad strokes it outlines your relevant work experience and any other essential information, hopefully starting to indicate the themes of who you are. It can stand on its own as a tool for you, but it can also work to complement a cover letter. The cover letter is the voice that talks directly to the employer. It expands on certain elements of the résumé and acts as the direct sale of your abilities.

The key to a good cover letter is specifics. The more specific you are, the more interesting you are—and the more the employer has a sense (as I've been pounding into you from Chapter 1) of who you are, what you've done, and how you did it. A cover letter has to stir up some interest in order to be remembered.

A friend of mine told me that at her job working at a racetrack she was handed a stack of forty résumés and asked to pick the people to be interviewed for a job opening. I asked her how she chose. "Well," she said, "only one of them really stuck out. It was kind of sweetly cheesy, but this one woman wrote in her cover letter that she loved Dick Francis mysteries and that it was her dream to work at a racetrack. It was the only one that was different. I felt as though I knew why she was applying and I put her in the interview pile." Just that little bit of information made the cover letter stick out from the rest. A little bit of vulnerability and realness signifying that a person was applying for the job instead of a robot.

Let's return to the plight of our friend from Chapter 2: Steve, Ruler of All Dishware. As I suggested when we were looking over his résumé and discovering a wide assortment of amazingly useful skills, Steve would be well suited for that first step in the business hierarchy, the mailroom. Many a rich and famous business person has begun a fabulous career there, and Steve has the advantage of already having all the required skills. Picture it: Steve in the mailroom discovers new ways to prioritize, sort, and organize the mail, and the mail flies faster around the office than ever before. One problem. How are we going to get an employer, some business-suited conservative type, to see the best in Steve? Let the cover letters roll. . . .

June 4, 1997

Dear Sir/Madam:

Please consider this letter and attached résumé as an application for employment with your organization.

As indicated in my résumé, I have accumulated two years of work experience in a variety of fields. In all the positions that I have held, I have proven to be an independent and conscientious worker. I take great pride in perfecting the skills required to deliver and maintain a high level of service to my employer. If given the opportunity to join your organization I will prove to be a fast learner and a dependable employee.

Thank you for your time and consideration. I look forward to meeting with you, at your convenience, to discuss further any opportunities that may be available.

Sincerely,

*Steve Santerini*

Steve Santerini

# The Standard Standard Letter

What do you think about the person who wrote this? The grammar and vocabulary are excellent. But beyond such stock phrases as "perfecting the skills" and "fast learner and dependable employee," what do we really know except that this version of Steve could be asking for a job as a grocery store manager, a junior stockbroker, or a cable guy? We're not sure. And further, I'm not sure if I can believe a guy who throws five-star phrases around so easily. At your most conservative, please don't head this route. This is the robot-style cover letter I was talking about earlier.

As tempting as it may be to use general, all-encompassing terms, none of them will hit home with a reader unless you demonstrate proof (yes, just like in the résumé) to back up your claims. Left unexplained, big-money terms like "successful" or "excellent" are awkward. Steve describes himself as a "proven" independent and conscientious worker. Who proved? How proved? Why should I believe him?

## 1. Just Like in a Résumé, Say Something Concrete

Mentioning your skills or the job you held isn't tangible enough to hold a reader's attention. Even the most conservative letter needs to follow this principle. Compare these two examples:

- *My people skills will be a valuable asset as a customer service representative, as demonstrated in my most recent job as a tour guide.*
- *In my last job as a tour guide for city hall, I not only narrated the city's stories, dramatized the historical information, and fielded questions, but I also tried to relate the information to the interests and age group of each specific tour. As a customer service representative I think my people skills would be a tremendous asset.*

See the difference? In the second example I can actually imagine this person doing the job.

In the résumé you're often stuck with just enough room for a run-down of the job and some proof that you did it well. The cover letter gives you the space to branch out, to elaborate on specific things. It's also a forum for making the connection between the skills of the last job and the skills you need for this new job.

Let's see how Steve does on his second try.

*June 4, 1997*

*Dear Sir/Madam*

*I am applying for your position of mailroom clerk. I am a quick learner, a good organizer, and a great team player. I have successfully used these skills in previous jobs and I believe that these skills, plus my ability to work well under pressure, are well suited to the position you offer. I would love to arrange a time when I could come talk to you about it.*

*I look forward to hearing from you.*

Sincerely

*Steve Santerini*

Steve Santerini

# The Standard Specific Letter

This letter is at least geared for the job at hand. What's your impression of this version of Steve? Does his letter strike you as the kind you'd keep for posterity after he's discovered as CBC's most trusted newscaster? Does it sound like the kind of letter you'd at least keep as an example for others to learn from? Does it even sound like the kind of letter you'd feel like reading all the way through?

Always keep your reader in mind. Employers have to look at a ton of these cover letters, and they're desperate for something interesting. Everyone who reads these letters is a practised skimmer. Your goal is to make them want to stop everything, read you all the way through, and then flip the page to that fantastic résumé.

The problem with the above letter is again its complete lack of substance, or at least in place of substance, personality. When I read the first line, "I am applying . . . ," I'm thinking "that's pretty obvious." By the next line, "I am a quick learner . . . ," I'm thinking "who cares?" and then Steve—wonderful, amazing, dishwashing Steve—is lost to me. Plus, this letter still suffers from the same generic skills problem of the first letter. How does Steve work with people? How does he know he's good at it? What constitutes "successful use of these skills"? For all I know, it means that Steve played well on the diner's baseball team. I just don't know Steve. I'm further turned off by Steve because he has no idea who I am either ("Dear Sir/Madam" just doesn't make me feel special).

## 2. Everything's a Cliché

I once had an English teacher named Mrs. Corbett, who made me a better writer by nailing me in red marker every time I used a clichéd phrase. Clichés are repetitive sentences or fragments that are commonly used by mass portions of the population to the point where they don't mean anything anymore. You may want to use phrases like these in your letter because it makes them "sound right." The reason they sound right is because they've been used by about twelve billion previous applicants. They're comfortable, well-worn, tired phrases, and they'll do you no favours in a stack of a hundred cover letters with similar phrases.

Avoid:

- *"I am applying for the position of . . ."*
- *"I am interested in the position of . . ."*
- *"I am responding to your ad of April 16th . . ."*
- *"I believe that my skills are demonstrated in my ability . . ."*

- *"I believe that my ability to organize would benefit your company . . ."*
- *"I feel strongly that this job . . ."*
- *". . . and I think your store would be a perfect fit with my skills!"*
- *"and I feel that my experience fits perfectly with your job opening . . ."*
- *". . . a perfect opportunity to use my skills to their fullest capacity"*
- *"This letter serves as an application . . ."*
- *"This work interests me, as I've had long practice . . ."*

Notice how one sentence fragment just kind of melts into the next. Trust me, managers and hiring staff have read them all before. They're not safe, they're boring, stale, and even irritating. If you're feeling really comfortable throwing huge phrases around, that's your warning sign that you're heading down the safe, already-said, don't-bother-reading-me route. The manager at the video store where I work saves his favourite creative cover letters. He didn't have any clichéd ones to show me (though he knew exactly what I meant) because he'd ditched them all. Write a cover letter the manager wants to keep.

Steve has been inspired by my words, and yet he's more fixated on saying something worthwhile than on watching his phrasing. Here's what Steve had to say.

June 4, 1997

Ms. Gruarin
Human Resources Manager
Pola Company Inc.
96 Simone Blvd.
Montreal, PQ
H5C 2E7

Dear Ms. Gruarin,

I am applying for the position of mailroom clerk in your office. I want you to know that although I've been a dishwasher and haven't worked in a mailroom before, I still think that I have much to contribute to your office environment.

As you will see on my résumé, I have been a member of many school teams at my high school, including soccer, hockey, baseball, and others. I have also organized a food drive for a local shelter that went for an entire year. I have always participated in these activities with enthusiasm, dedication, commitment, and a strong sense of the team-oriented approach that you would want in an office worker.

As for the dishwashing jobs, I feel that over time I have learned much from these experiences in terms of the responsibility they have required. I had to successfully manage many difficult situations, particularly at the restaurant, which has enabled me to find ways of looking for solutions other than the obvious. Rather than hurting my chance to do this job for you, I feel that my experiences have in fact benefited me, and I am actually more prepared to work for you as a result.

In conclusion I know that I would be an asset to your organization, and that I could also learn from the work. I seek to understand and further myself in every job that I take. I wish to do the same with you. I would love for you to contact me so that we could discuss this further. I look forward to hearing from you.

Sincerely

*Steve Santerini*

Steve Santerini

# The Extended Let-Me-Tell-You-Everything Letter

This is a really good try. It addresses Steve's weaknesses, explains his activities, and sounds incredibly genuine. It might—might—even get some responses. But we know Steve, and we know that he's more interesting than this. It's not that I doubt the sincerity of the message, or that I don't know more about what this Steve does than I do in the other letters. The problem here is that Steve drags out his experiences, but never says anything about what happened. He refers to difficult situations (in the restaurant in particular) as if I should understand, but I wasn't there so how can I get this nudge, wink, "you know what I mean"? I don't. And Steve doesn't make me care. How did the job benefit you? What skills did you actually demonstrate and how? What does it matter to me if you won't tell me? Further, he continues to refer to his own "learning," which makes me wonder if he knows the difference between a job and math class.

Despite his willingness to demonstrate how he could be useful, Steve still sounds as though he's smaller and weaker than he really is. I want to know exactly what I'd get if I hired Steve, not just a run-down of things he's done.

## 3. Show Yourself with at Least One Sentence

Even if all of this still feels as though I'm asking the world of you, do me one favour. Make sure that you put in at least one line that reflects you personally. Remember the student who liked horse race mysteries? She landed in the interview pile because in that one line she showed more of her true self than anyone else in the stack.

## 4. Read It Over and Envision the Reader

We all want the reader of the letter to be impressed. And indeed, making an impression is very important. But what I'm asking you to shoot for instead is making the reader *interested* in you. Let's face it, unless you're my roommate (who's landed at least five jobs from her cover letters alone), you and I aren't going to be getting a job off our cover letter. What we're looking for is a response. A flicker of interest. Anything that will make them check out the résumé, put us in the yes pile, and give us a call. Therefore interesting them, rather than impressing them, is the key. Make them want to meet you.

## 5. Demonstrate Confidence in Your Ability to Handle the Job

When Steve says "I still think I have something to offer," it's as though he's predicting from the first paragraph that we won't believe him. He *knows* he can do the job, so why is he apologizing? There's tremendous power in approaching people believing that they'll value what you have to say. Invite them to consider you in the most positive way possible. Everyone wants to tell you that people are only out to get you. Look, if they don't value your opinion of yourself, you don't want to work there. So approach them with a strong sense of your own value to their organization, and believe that they'll see you that way too. If they don't respond positively, good riddance.

With these ideas in mind, let's check out Steve's next attempt, in which he tries to be way more interesting.

*June 4, 1997*

*Ms. Gruarin*
*Human Resources Manager*
*Pola Company Inc.*
*96 Simone Blvd.*
*Montreal, PQ*
*H5C 2E7*

*Dear Ms. Gruarin,*

*I am applying to work in your mailroom, and I'm writing to tell you that I can "deliver" the goods—literally! Mail is my life. I'm a cheery, hard-working, responsible kind of guy and I just know that your work environment will benefit from my presence. You want to hire me! I'll give Santa Claus a run for his money!*

*Give me a ring, if you want me to do the mail thing.*

*Ciao!*

*Steve Santerini*

*Steve Santerini*

## The "Aren't I Wacky," Saying Nothing/Irritating Everyone Letter

Oops. Too far the other way. This guy has loads of personality, but the kind that would have you calling the firing squad rather than the hiring squad. His confidence is lodged in nothing that I can grab hold of and the humour gets in the way of the message. When you're looking to write a cover letter, even to the most non-traditional and creative company in town, totally casual never flies.

Once again, Steve has said nothing that proves to me that I want to speak to him about his previous experience. The difference is that I'll remember this letter—as the one I threw away after shaking my head at it. This kind of letter has the same effect as those commercials that are so irritating that you remember the store just because the annoying salesperson drilled the name into you. Whether or not this technique actually works for furniture sales, I can pretty much guarantee you that it won't work when selling yourself. I read this and think "cheesy guy," which is not the kind of message you want to be sending out to future employers.

Further, humour is a tricky element in writing a cover letter. People will tell you never to use humour, or at most to use it sparingly and subtly. I believe there's a definite difference between the forced humour that comes from trying to be funny, and letting humour develop naturally out of a situation or idea. Run it by someone who will tell you the truth. Remember who your audience is. And any humour that requires an exclamation mark is probably out.

## 6. Being Creative Doesn't Mean You Have to Be a Creative Writer

There are a number of ways to make your cover letter stand out. You could start by asking a question which you answer by the end of the letter. You could use an interesting or relevant quotation, maybe on the company, from a newspaper article, say, and then jump right in and tell the reader why you think the quote is applicable to them hiring you. You can talk about the company rather than yourself. Remember that your résumé is lying right underneath your cover letter, so don't feel obliged to repeat what you've already said.

For instance, one applicant to *Toronto Life* magazine discussed the things that he associated with Toronto, and why he liked the city. It made for a different read, and gave the letter a more outwardly focused feel. Another cover letter addressed an issue the company was facing, and the writer's ideas about what it would mean for the business. Then she mentioned where she felt she could make a contribution. In each of these cases the writer wasn't the next Jerry Seinfeld, but each letter made an impact by being thoughtful, interesting, and different.

So let's take a look at how a cover letter can be both straightforward and interesting.

June 4, 1997

Ms. Gruarin
Human Resources Manager
Pola Company Inc.
96 Simone Blvd.
Montreal, PQ
H5C 2E7

Dear Ms. Gruarin,

Despite the "dishwashing only" experience on my résumé, my work and personality skills directly match the job of mailroom office clerk.

I organize: At the restaurant there are 6 different kinds of glasses, 7 different kinds of cutlery, 4 kinds of plates, 2 kinds of cups, and assorted kitchenware. I keep all of this chaos under control, both before, when they're heaped in dirty piles and have to be sorted for cleaning, and afterwards, when they must be stacked in special racks and trays.

I prioritize: To keep necessary items in stock out front so that customers have one of everything to eat with, I keep constant watch over the different loads going into the machines, in order to have the right amount of each load ready in the prep area for the waiters to take.

I communicate: To stay efficient, I check with the wait staff to address their concerns and daily needs. In turn, I ask them to do a little up front work so that I can return clean dishes to them faster. This method of give and take creates a strong teamwork component to my job.

These are just some of the skills that are infinitely applicable to the mailroom. Let's talk about some more.

Sincerely,

*Steve Santerini*

Steve Santerini

## The Three-Part Skill Demonstration Letter

So clear! I don't have to do any re-reading, close reading, or mind reading to know what skills Steve has. He's demonstrated proof that these skills exist, and the small details that he adds help me to envision his job. The details are things like the number of glasses, or the description of the dishes before they're cleaned. There's even a subtle humour in these kinds of details, maybe not the laugh out loud kind, but the quick smile kind. And even if the employer skims the letter, all the points are laid out so easily that I could still get a great impression of Steve on a fly-by read.

Note how Steve addresses his limited work experience at the outset, and uses it to his advantage as a lead-in to the rest of the letter. He takes his weakness and makes it an advantage, and that makes him more interesting.

### 7. The Rule of Three

In your résumé you don't want to be trying to highlight twelve fabulous skills at once, even though you may have—in fact you probably do have—twelve fabulous skills that *could* be highlighted. The cover letter is where you get choosy and find the ones that really match the job description. Any more than three and you're overwhelming your reader with too much information. (Flip to the skills list at the end of this book to help you zero in on specific attributes.)

### 8. The Rule of Three, Part Two

The cover letter is usually no more than three paragraphs. If the application request requires more information, by all means chat away. But if your letter is deviating off into page two and onwards, give it a rest. Nine times out of ten you'll sell yourself better if you're short and snappy, not long-winded.

### 9. Address the Weakness Up Front

All the reader has to do is turn the page to find out that your experience doesn't directly match the job description. Say that in your first line. The positive aspect of your weakness is that it gives you a great place to start your letter and actually makes it an interesting read once you've put the problem out there. Don't finish your letter until you've discussed how your weakness can be overcome. It's not just a matter of pointing it out; you must also provide the proof that you have the skills to overcome it.

## 10. Conservative Letter Writers Can Stop Here

If Steve's last letter appeals to you, this is the kind of style you should stick to. You can say something clear, precise, and to the point. You can say something a little more personal, but nothing too out there. No crazy storytelling. No weird jokes. But if you think this letter is good but lacks the essence of your true personality, move on.

Meanwhile, Steve tries his hand at another variation on the precise and direct style of cover letter.

June 4, 1997

Ms. Gruarin
Human Resources Manager
Pola Company Inc.
96 Simone Blvd.
Montreal, PQ
H5C 2E7

Dear Ms. Gruarin,

What does a mailroom have to do with washing dishes?

Good question, and one that I ask myself every time I pull a tray of steaming hot cutlery from the dishwashing machine at the busy diner where I work.

Having given it much thought—between collecting loads of dirty dishes from the front, sorting cutlery into their correct piles, organizing the mounds of dishes into specific racks, prioritizing loads so that waiters don't run out of any one item, and delivering the clean goods during rushes when wait staff can't get to the dishroom—I've decided that the two jobs might be quite similar.

What I do: collecting, sorting, organizing, prioritizing, and delivering, which is what I envision happening in your mailroom. I'm very proud of my work in the dishroom, but I'm ready to retire my apron. I look forward to hearing from you.

Sincerely,

*Steve Santerini*

Steve Santerini

# The Answering a Question Letter

Steve successfully pulls off two strategies at once. First, as we noted in the last section, he addresses his weakness from the start, and finds a convincing way to demonstrate that the skills needed are exactly the same for both jobs. Further, he asks a question at the beginning that he knows how to answer. The question serves as his teaser to coax Ms. Gruarin to read the whole letter to find out the answer. Catchy, isn't it?

## 11. Cut to the Chase

Make your letter active rather than passive. Eliminate wordy phrasings like "as a matter of fact," or even "for example." Jump right into the action. Who are you? What have you been doing? Why do you want to work at this place? Answer these questions directly because the extra padding, while making you feel safe, bores the reader.

## 12. Address It Correctly

For any good cover letter to work its magic, it has to be sent to someone specific. Sometimes this is easy—a mere matter of looking at the name on the employment ad, or a breezy chat with a friendly receptionist. Sometimes it's harder, requiring you to do some fancy legwork. But it's always worth it, whatever you do. People tend to feel more obliged to read something if it has their name on it. That only makes sense. It's easy not to feel responsible when the letter on your desk says "Dear Sir/Madam" or "To whom it may concern." Even if it lands on the wrong desk, that person will either pass it on to the right person or contact you. Either way, it gives you an in to the company, and in some cases may find you a champion from an unexpected corner.

And like the résumé, bad layout can ruin brilliant content. You want to address the letter in the proper business-letter style. You need the date, your name, address, and phone number, and then the name, title, address, and phone (and fax) number of the person to whom you're sending the letter. Including all this information in a clear layout helps give a sense of professionalism and completion to the page.

The date, your stuff, and their stuff can go all on the left, or you can have the date and you on the right and then the other person on the left. Just as long as it's correct and consistent.

## 13. Check Your Spelling

Just as you did for your résumé, give your cover letter a going over for spelling, punctuation, and any other tiny detail errors.

Here's a tip: "résumé," as you may have noticed, is spelled with two accented é's—something that a lot of people get wrong. (You can add accents on a Mac computer by pressing option and "e," then "e" alone. If you're stuck, use a fine black marker.) I once heard about a woman at a publishing company who was looking for a new editor. She was deluged with résumés, and reduced the pile by throwing out, regardless of content, all those with cover letters that spelled "résumé" without the accents. Given that editors should know better, it was an effective method of elimination. Don't be ruled out because poor spelling made your first impression look sloppy.

Steve has practised with the last two formats and he likes them a lot. But Steve's creative side is aching to be heard, so he goes for a cover letter that has more storytelling involved.

June 4, 1997

Steve Santerini
4852 Av. du Parc
Montreal, PQ
H2V 4E6
279-4754

Ms. Gruarin
Human Resources Manager
Pola Company Inc.
96 Simone Blvd.
Montreal, PQ
H5C 2E6

Dear Ms. Gruarin,

I want to work in your mailroom. My problem is this: my last two major jobs were as a dishwasher. My solution is simple. I'm guessing you want someone who can sort, organize, prioritize, anticipate, and deliver. This is the motto of the dishroom.

On Thanksgiving day I was working the 10 a.m. to 8 p.m. shift. I had piles and racks and trays of clean dishes and cutlery coming out of the dishwasher, ready to go. I had separated the cutlery, I'd organized the cups and saucers, and I'd sorted out the racks of pop, alcohol, and water glasses. Everything was ready for the waiters to come pick up as usual. But a half hour had passed since the last one had come in. I grabbed a load of each, glasses too, and headed to the serving area. Every waiter was on the floor, madly clearing and serving, and the manager was in the kitchen trying to help the cook. She stopped prepping six turkey dinners long enough to tell me I was a life saver.

Let me be your life saver.

*Steve Santerini*

Steve Santerini

## The Specific Incident Letter

I don't know about you, but I had a clear vision of Steve on Thanksgiving day. I have a particular image of the moment Steve walks from his quiet, organized dish-room into the bedlam out front. By placing the reader at the heart of a busy day, Steve allows us inside his job. Mrs. Corbett, the no-clichés English teacher I told you about, had another saying: "Show me, don't tell me." Don't tell me that the manager was very busy and thanked you for your foresight in bringing out needed dish-ware—show me. This example would have earned Steve an A from Mrs. Corbett.

Right away I want to say that if this letter leaves you shaky, go back to the last two and use them as your starting point. These next two letters are for students who are confident storytellers only. It's more than okay if you don't like this style. That's the essence of personality: more than one style. If this kind of letter is unleashing the creative writer in your head, read on so that you'll still be writing a cover letter, not a novelette.

## 14. You Watched *Full House,* Didn't You?

You know when you're home alone and you end up watching those tacky sitcoms or bad TV movies? I don't know if this happens to you, but if I watch only a little bit, I get drawn into what the family will do about that wacky Urkel, just one more time. Why do I get suckered in? It's a sociological fact that humans have a hard time resisting the pull of a narrative. Our natural curiosity kicks in and we want to know what happens. A story is a powerful tool in the hands of a decent storyteller.

You can use this principle to your advantage when writing a cover letter. Whether you're talking about a specific incident, charting your growth through a job you had, or even describing how you handled rowdy dogs as a vet assistant, you can turn a letter into a spellbinding slice of your life. Regardless of what they first think, readers will be drawn into reading your whole letter. Then they may want to peek at the person behind the story and check out your résumé. Bingo.

## 15. Create Balance in Your Letter

What do I mean by balance? If you take the very direct tone with which you begin the letter and keep it up throughout, it may feel like too much. The middle part of the letter (the big, crazy story) is actually the more relaxed part. Having loosened up through the body of the letter, you can leave off a little more kookily ("Let me be your life saver"). That line wouldn't work if the whole letter took that tone. You can also switch the type of balance. You could start the letter off in a more conservative fashion, have a direct, specific middle, and then return to a more conservative tone at the end. What you're looking to do is to stay away from a "wacky" letter while still presenting yourself differently. Try this out, and then ask someone else (who has a liberal cover letter outlook) what they think.

Steve has another idea for a storytelling type letter.

June 4, 1997

Steve Santerini
4852 Av. du Parc
Montreal, PQ
H2V 4E6
279-4754

Ms. Gruarin
Human Resources Manager
Pola Company Inc.
96 Simone Blvd,
Montreal, PQ
H5C 2E7

Dear Ms. Gruarin,

I started at Norm's Diner as a busboy, but two weeks later the weekend dishwasher called in sick and I had to take over. By the end of the day I had broken fifteen pieces of restaurant property, taken ten years off each waiter's life, and was considering eating off paper plates for the rest of my natural-born existence.

The manager came to tell me that I'd been permanently promoted; Moynul, the original dishwasher, would not be returning any time soon. I was jealous of Moynul. Not wanting a repeat of my first-day fun, I initially ran myself ragged just to keep up to pace, juggling bus pans, sorting cutlery, scraping plates, doing anything—anything possible—to have whatever the waiters needed ready to go. But I never seemed to get it done quickly enough, or I'd cleaned too many of the saucers when they were all out of cutlery.

I went into heavy-duty assimilation time. I learned the ways of the dishroom, the workings of the machine, and how to prioritize all the different loads of dishware, glasses, and cutlery so that the hottest items like cutlery were always available. Most importantly though, I learned to work with the waiters so that I didn't need to ask them what they needed, but instead to anticipate, and sometimes even bring it out for them. In turn, they listened to my requests to organize and clear their dishes in the dish pans, making my job easier and the whole process faster.

In the interests of myself, and Moynul, who wants his job back, I would love to work for you in the mailroom. I will be available at the above number to discuss that possibility further.

Sincerely,

*Steve Santerini*

Steve Santerini

## The Showing Growth through Movement Letter

Again, it's the small details that bring this description to life. Even Moynul takes on a personality of his own. The fact that Steve was breaking dishware his first day works as a foil to how things actually turned out. Notice how the letter comes full circle, creating a balance between beginning and ending, and how even the type of humour remains the same. This kind of story is gentler than the slam, whiz, bang of the previous one. And when Steve states in his résumé that the owner wants him to work full time, it acts as further proof that this dishwashing disaster was crowned the king.

### 16. You Don't Want to Be *Full House* Though, Do You?

When you're telling the story it's the small details that move it from sitcom-y, fake-laugh land to feature-length, millions-grossing material. It's the difference between what "usually" happens and what "did" happen—and you were actually there and there weren't any cute twins playing your sister. Make the story in the comparisons between then and now, before and after, what should have and what did happen. Whatever the scene or the overall feeling may be, think of all the details that will help the reader become even more absorbed. You want him or her to be able to envision the scenario.

Small details, like adjectives describing the state of your shirt the first day you finished construction work, or your favourite song you sang to campers at night to help them sleep, make you sound like a real person. A description of a customer you helped, or how you handled a pool full of five-year-old monster children, can be the juice of your cover letter—and the compelling reason why the reader will want to get to know who you are.

Do you remember the movie *Silence of the Lambs?* When the mother's on TV pleading with the killer to release her daughter, she repeats her daughter's name over and over. Clarice tells her roommate that that's to help the killer see the victim as a person, and thus make it harder for him to kill her. The FBI uses this technique, and I encourage you to do the same. It's harder to "kill" the résumé of someone who sounds like a real person. I don't mean for you to write your name a million times in your letter, but I do want you to write in a little bit of your personality.

### 17. Be Brave

It takes tremendous courage to do any of this stuff, especially for the first time. People three times your age still get shaky when they have to write a cover letter. *I* get shaky when I have to write a cover letter. I respect the fact that this process draws upon all your self-esteem and you ain't gonna be lovin' every minute of it. Stick with it. Keep the faith, your job is out there.

So there you have it. Steve has four fabulous choices of a cover letter, depending on how he feels, the company he's applying to, or which way the wind is blowing.

## A Very Important Word of Warning

The cover letter writing techniques I've outlined here are wonderful to use when the person to whom you're writing has no idea who you are and could care less unless you jump out of the page and do a tap dance on their desk. But when the person to whom you're sending a cover letter knows who you are, or knows of you from a close contact, the tone of the letter has to change somewhat.

If the cover letter is just a formality, you can stick with a much more traditional-sounding letter. I still think that you should back up your skills and show a little personality, but the wacky, attention-getting, fun stuff can take a breather. The difference is that in this case the person knows your personality, so you don't have to sell, sell, sell. It's more respectful to take it easy.

If the cover letter is being sent to someone who doesn't know you, but you're being recommended by a contact, the same exception to the rule holds true. And that makes sense, because if Aunt Jane is your contact, the other person won't refuse to consider your letter. Again, less "hit 'em over the head to stand out" is a good plan, but don't divest your letter of all personality or proof. Always mention the contact name in your letter, so that the person is aware that you're no ordinary applicant and will know who to ask about you. Remember to check with the person before you use their name to get you in the door.

So now you've got your résumé and your cover letter, printed out and ready to go. Congratulations, and welcome to the next step.

CHAPTER 4

# Scams, Schemes, and All Things in Between

We're now in the limbo land between your résumé and cover letter and actually looking for work. In the next chapter we'll address how to actually go outside of the house and get a job, but in the meantime, here's stuff to think about while squeezing in that last day of Oprah-watching before you have to get your butt moving toward the door.

Since this chapter may seem to contain a mishmash of subject matter, let me give you a run-down of the contents so that you can decide what you want to read. First up is the exciting stuff: the people who want to scam you, and what could happen if you try to scam other people. Then comes the more sedate but still essential information on how to deal with references and thank-you letters. We'll round out the chapter by discussing Social Insurance Numbers, library research, and then (if you're still awake) end with a few tips on how to check out the Net.

## The Bare Minimum

Do you know what the minimum wage is in your province? It can be anywhere from $4.75 (P.E.I.) to $7 an hour (Northwest Territories). For workers under the age of eighteen the minimum wage is usually around 40 or 50 cents less than the regular minimum. The best way to find out your provincial minimum wage is to ask at a government employment agency. And remember that these figures do change, so it's worth checking them from time to time.

Employers must pay you minimum wage, which means that if you're getting paid less you can complain (ask the employment centre where) and force them to give you back-pay to make up the difference.

There are a few exceptions. The wait staff at restaurants often get paid less ($4 to $5.95 an hour), since management knows that with their tips waiters will end up earning more than the minimum. Camp jobs are low-paying, particularly if you're sixteen and under. And if you're under fifteen and you're doing something like babysitting, which isn't regulated, you'll probably have to settle for less. But then again, what are you worried about? You don't have to fill the car with gas and you don't have to learn cosign in math class yet. Relax and enjoy your job.

If they aren't paying you $6.40 or $6.85 an hour but you're doing regular work, then you have a problem. Sometimes employers are hoping that you don't know the minimum, and if you do, some might try to convince you that it's okay for this particular job. You'll have to make the call on whether it's worth the battle, or if the job is worth the pay. If you're being paid a lump sum and they hold back vacation pay, that isn't allowed either. Note also if you're paying more than five percent income tax. You shouldn't have to because students are exempt from certain taxes. Another way that employers try to scam you is by not paying you overtime. Check what your rights are in this matter by reviewing the company policy (probably holed up in a binder somewhere).

If you're facing any of these dilemmas, you can go to your provincial Ministry of Labour or to your local youth (or regular) human resources centre. The counsellors there will help you figure out what to do. Meanwhile, if something smells fishy before you take the job, trust your instincts and ask questions. Better to find out you're being scammed now rather than halfway through July when there are a lot fewer job prospects.

## How Not to Get Rich Quick

When an actual job is a scam it may do more than just leave you stranded—it might rip you off entirely. These "get a job quick" schemes can waste a day or your whole summer. The Better Business Bureau for your area will help you determine the legitimacy of the jobs you apply for.

Scams can range from "work-abroad" schemes that promise guaranteed jobs that don't exist in far-away countries, to "information packages" that are advertised as including job offers and get $500 from applicants who receive only lists of companies, some of which are out of business. Number one note: no real job offer would ever have you send money to them. If you think it's legit, but they're asking for money up front, call the Better Business Bureau first.

Really, if any deal sounds too good to be true, particularly if it's being promoted in a public place, it probably is. Being paid to monitor a computer or phone at home, overseas jobs advertised in newspapers, part-time work making crafts or stuffing envelopes, high-income sales positions requiring no experience that are promised in newspaper ads or over the phone, or anything that smacks of "get rich quick" should be avoided, or at least approached with sense and caution.

Another way you can be suckered are schemes where you make a percentage off selling a product for someone. Now if you're working for a legitimate company with offices and a variety of products, that's door-to-door work. But if your "dealer" is working out of his or her own home, wants you to invest in the product up front, and refuses to let you see the goods, be warned. This may sound far-fetched, but similar stories have been covered each year in the news.

Finally, there's the infamous pyramid sales scam. The basic principle is that you sell a product, recruit others to sell the product, and then make money off of them and anyone else they recruit. The variations can include person-to-person sales, schemes that require a certified cheque for $1000-plus for your very own video-selling program, and even fairly legitimate-looking businesses with regular business people trying to elude the rat race.

## The Lying Game

You've probably already heard stories of people who got jobs 'cause they lied about their experience, their references, or some other bit of crucial information. I know people who've lied, and instead of sitting in juvy they're working their butts off at decent jobs. But I'm uncomfortable about lying. I was terrible at trying not to get carded, so why would I be any better at lying in a job situation? Furthermore, I'm more comfortable explaining my own experiences, not fictionalized ones. In Chapter 6 I explain how to knock 'em dead by describing specific examples of your experience. It's easy to say "I've waitered before." But when you've never done the job it's much harder to answer questions like "What kind of order system did you use?" "How much food did you sell each week?" or "Tell me about a specific time you helped a customer." I believe that an unquestionable sincerity and enthusiasm comes through when you talk about your own experience. Employers are practised b.s. sniffers, and can hear the note of genuineness in your voice.

Sometimes lying will get you the job, but once you take it the consequences could be severe. For instance, one student I know told a school board that was hiring maintenance workers that she'd had a painting job, when in truth she'd helped out one day on someone else's crew. The first day on the job her boss told her to go to the store and buy all the materials and enough paint to cover an entire school. Our student panicked, called a friend who'd done the work before, and got a crash course in "how to paint a school." The job turned out all right, but had she made a mistake based on her inexperience she'd have cost her employer a lot of money and herself a job.

Now, you could argue that there's a difference between outright lying and learning on the job. Take my friend, whom I've since dubbed "Jungle Judy." Judy was once an anthropology student, and thought it would be a good idea to learn Spanish in Ecuador. Around the time that she was supposed to come home, she convinced the owner of a jungle lodge near the rain forest to take her on as a naturalist guide. Judy quickly learned the tricks of the trade to get her out of trouble when she didn't know the answer to the tourists' pesky questions. Starting each tour with "We still don't know ninety percent of what the rain forests hold," Jungle Judy was off the hook for answering any pressing questions about unfamiliar insect groups or odd-looking plant life.

One day, paddling along the Napo River in the Amazon Basin, Judy was growing tired of answering "I don't know" to every question when a particularly interested tourist asked her if Ecuador had any manatee. Manatee are the kind, gentle sea cows (walruses without tusks or attitude), that are too slow and stupid to get out of the way of speeding boats, causing their unfortunate disappearance from Floridian waterways and unfortunate reappearance on the endangered species list. Judy had never heard of manatee before. But rather than admit that salient detail, she grabbed her binoculars and started scanning the skies for manatee. The tourist watched her, perplexed, until he finally interrupted her skyward search for sea mammals and tried again, "I said manatee." "Oh," said Judy, getting the hint and putting down the binoculars, "I thought you said Black Neo-Tropical Cormorant," which sounds somewhat similar if you put the stress on a different vowel.

Judy got away with keeping her job while being almost completely ignorant of the knowledge it required (she once convinced several grade six biology teachers that algae, a one-celled plant organism, actually jumped off three-toed sloths to lay their eggs—did I mention that Judy is a very credible liar?). But over the year and a half that she did the job, Judy learned all you ever wanted to know about insect and plant life. She even went so far as to consume a large, living, bright green katydid (it looks like a cricket only bigger and it struggled all the way down) to show her dedication to the pursuit of intimate knowledge about these creatures (well, okay, it was a dare).

Remember that lying is, in essence, breaking trust with someone who may become your employer and maybe even your friend. Once you put that lie out there, you have to be prepared to go where it takes you. If you think you can handle that, and feel that you won't get a job any other way, I'm not going to argue with you. I do hope that you'll take the safety of others into consideration; for instance lying about lifesaving credentials when little kids are involved, or driving abilities where cars are involved. And that's all I'm going to say on the subject 'cause I ain't your mama.

# References--
# Who, How, and Why?

Remember that little line in Chapter 2 about "references on request"? I didn't want to worry you about it then, but the time has come to make that line come true.

The point of a reference is to make sure that someone else can vouch for the places you've worked and the type of person you are. It functions as both a double check on what you said in your résumé, and as further information for an employer trying to make a decision. If someone is considering you seriously, good references tend to put you over the top. Also, an employer can ask reference-specific kinds of questions from an employer-y viewpoint. Some employers never call references, some call all and ask in-depth questions, and some just call to find out if they've ever heard of you.

I can hear the worry in your voice. "I've never worked before," "I got fired from my last job," "I think my boss hates me," "I don't know where my phone is." Take a deep breath, I'm still here with you.

## 1. References don't have to be from bosses who paid you a salary.

I'm sure that some of you out there are breathing a sigh of relief. Almost anybody can be used as a reference, as long as he or she can vouch for your abilities and believes in you. It could be a teacher, a parent you babysat for, a friend of the family. It can be someone you worked one day for, or someone you volunteered for. It could even be one of your parents, but only if you've worked for them at their office, say, or place of business.

## 2. That being said, it's helpful if at least one of your references was your employer.

Potential employers love to hear about you from their own kind. No matter how many great personal references you can dig up, at least one person should have hired you in the past, even if the duration of your job was as minimal as your pay. All employers want to hear is that you can handle the conditions of employment—that you showed up on time, followed directions, and didn't lose the children. A mother you babysat for or a neighbour whose walk you shovelled can count. If you're really stuck, go to your local youth employment centre. Sometimes they organize events that can get you work for a day or two and get you a reference.

## 3. That being said, it's even more helpful if at least one of your references knows your abilities as related to the job you're applying for.

It'd be great if you were applying to be a landscape and gardening crew member and had three glowing references from three different bosses for whom you did wonderful things with their azaleas. But given your age and stage, that scenario isn't very likely. The best thing to do is give as professional a reference as you can, say a former employer for whom you babysat or sold carpet cleaning products. Then combine that with a reference from a neighbour whose garden you tended while they were away. They may not have paid you anything and were only gone for two weeks, but if they were happy with their lawn they're a legitimate and relevant reference for the job at hand. The combination of these references shows that you know something about lawn care and something about how to work for an employer. Let them do the math.

## 4. You need more than one reference, but fewer than six.

Potential bosses find it much more reassuring to hear from at least two different people that you're a safe bet. If you're fourteen and have only one work-related reference, this is the time to reread key point number one and think of someone else, like a teacher or family friend who knows you're not a schmuck and that you can handle weeding lawns. However, if you're Joe/Josephine Superstar and you have ten people who want to say good things about you, prune down the list, will you? No one will ever call all those people anyway, and if they do they'll probably resent it. The standard number of references is three—two former employers and someone personal. You can choose what references to keep based on the next key point.

## 5. Ask permission first.

It's only polite to get in touch with people before you actually use them as references. This is easier to do if the person you want to use as a reference has seen or spoken to you recently. (So if you find someone who knows you quite well and thinks you're amazing—hold on for a mind-blowing proposition—stay in touch with them!) Asking their permission is a thoughtful way of reminding them what a superstar you are. Call them up and say, "I'm in the process of applying for job as a vet assistant. Would it be possible to list you as a reference?" The other bonus of asking first is that you can confirm that the person will give you a positive reference. If you just hand out the number without checking first, you lose control over what the person will say. If you ask first, you give the person room to say "I'd love to," or "I don't think that would be a good idea, given that my only clear memory of you is the time you tortured my dog."

## 6. Give them the power to give you a good reference.

More than just asking permission, you want to help your contact give you a kick-ass reference by reminding them what you've done and explaining what you'll be applying for. This is particularly true of more personal references, such as teachers or peer counsellors. You could say something like "I'm applying for a job as an assistant bookkeeper at Periscope book store. They're looking for someone who's responsible, good with figures, and an effective team worker. I thought that since you saw me balance the money for the school band's trip to Florida, you could mention those kinds of qualities." Often your references will ask you what they should say, so think about which of your skills should be highlighted.

If you haven't spoken to the person in a while and you've done other applicable jobs in the meantime, you could mention that to them too. And if you know who'll be calling them, tell them the name so that they'll know to respond immediately.

## 7. Jobs that didn't work out don't have to show up on reference lists.

Everybody screws up at least one job on their way to figuring out how to handle "adult responsibility" (remember what we said about checking in with the reference *before* handing out their number). You have some options.

First, if you have other strong references, and it's just your most recent job that went badly, leave it off. You don't have to include everyone who ever hired you anyway (key point #5). If, however, you don't include any work-related references and you've had twelve different jobs in the last two years, it looks a little suspicious. (Warning: If it's always their fault and you've said that twelve times, you may want to reassess your perspective and ask yourself some tough questions. A good start would be "What responsibility can I take for things not working out over and over again?") Re-adjust your résumé, selecting only a few prominent jobs and listing as references only those people who believe in you, even if they aren't work-related.

If you need to include a job because leaving it out would be too obvious, you either have to make sure the reference will still be okay, or you have to honestly address the problem in the interview, particularly if the interviewer brings it up. *If you have to discuss it*, don't blame your previous employer, take responsibility for your part in the problem (not all of it, your part), and let the employer infer the rest. Always say what you did well as well as what you didn't. Describing how you've matured since then can work wonders, particularly if you can demonstrate any kind of positive growth.

### 8. Adjust your reference list for each job.

It's also a good idea to adjust your references the way you'd adjust your résumé. If you apply for a different kind of job, you may want to put one reference down instead of another. Or you could simply rearrange the order to emphasize a particular person first. This doesn't mean that you always have to rearrange things. It just means that in the psychological game of getting an interview or job, you always have to be thinking as each particular employer will. This includes putting first someone they may know, or someone who might carry weight for another reason.

## Laying Out "References on Request"

A simple layout, neatly typed, on a separate sheet of paper, will suffice. The best bet is to bring your list to the interview (that's when they'll most likely ask for it anyway). You could also use it to boost your applicability when you're handing someone your résumé ("I've included my references if you're interested").

This is the least flashy part of the résumé package. Professional-looking is key, as it lends a sense of legitimacy to the information. It's a nice touch to include the title of your reference. Where it's important, you could also note if the reference is a personal one or work-related. A further nice touch is to include your references' available hours, particularly for those people who are hard to reach.

## Theng You, Theng You Verrah Mush

You want the inside track on how to stay on the good side of every potential contact, reference, and employer? Write them a thank-you letter. This is the quiet art of the job hunt. It's a way of both acknowledging someone's help and reminding them of what you talked about. Many people leave out this step, which is a bonus for you because you'll look even better when you send one. And if you look good, I look good.

You could thank a reference by letter, although it's sometimes nicer to call. For their part, they just want to know that they were in some way helpful and that you're in some way employed. And by calling them you'll probably also get to hear what they said, which is nice, and they'll feel encouraged to help you the next time you need a job (don't fool yourself—this job process thing happens a lot in a lifetime).

Thanking a contact is an absolute must, particularly when the person is high on the hiring chain, puts aside the time to ask you questions and give you advice, and/or puts you on to other people. That probably includes everyone you talked to.

Thanking a potential employer may be suited for some jobs more than others, but if you've gone through a hiring process, a series of interviews, or anything that took some time and will take some time before you get the results, write a follow-up letter that thanks them for considering you, and outlines one or two things you might have talked about in your interview.

Keep the letter short, sweet, and to the point. For example:

Dear Ms. Rovari,

I wanted to write and thank you for spending the time on the phone with me the other day. I needed to understand how the magazine business worked, and you've made the process much clearer. I'll be following up with the names you gave me and I'll let you know how it goes. If you ever start that gourmet magazine we talked about, and you need to hire cheap but labour-intensive staff, you can start with me!

Thanks again,

*Pearl Highland*

Pearl Highland

Another ballsy trick is to go to the person's office (particularly if it's a contact you've never met, only spoken to on the phone) and ask to "put the letter in their hands." Tell the receptionist that you don't have an appointment, but that you only need a minute if the person's available. When the person comes around the corner, introduce yourself: "Hi, I'm Pearl Highland, I spoke to you on the phone the other day. I just wanted to deliver this letter to you and see you briefly in person. Thanks again." Then leave. It has the same effect as when an obviously interested date doesn't jump you on the first night. There's nothing like doing something unexpectedly cool to make people remember who you are.

## Social Insurance Number --A Job Hunting Must

There's one essential item you'll need if you want to get paid. (I thought that might get your attention.) If you don't already have one, get yourself a social insurance card before you even start filling out applications and writing résumés.

To do so, go to your local Canada Employment Centre and fill out an application form. You'll need your birth certificate. If you're from Quebec, a baptismal certificate will do. If you're from Newfoundland, a baptismal or a dedication certificate will suffice. You'll also need a second piece of ID. It could be a driver's licence, or a report card from school—anything will do as long as it has your name on it. If you were born outside of Canada you'll need your Canadian Citizenship card, Immigration 1000 form, or passport with your Landed Immigrant stamp.

It'll take about four weeks to receive your card through the mail. (Remember that you're dealing with the government and the Canadian postal service. Snail mail and the Feds do not necessarily add up to quick postage.) Plan ahead, and get the card before you start looking for jobs.

## How to Be a Bookworm

I know what you're thinking. "Karen, why do I, not even graduated, have to do an adult thing like library research in order to get a job?" There are of course certain kinds of jobs that don't lend themselves to research. But if you're trying to get a job where knowledge in a certain area is important, you need to know where to look. It may be anything from the name and phone number of every film company in your province, to whatever information on the Gap you can use when you're applying for a job there, to the specifics of World Wide Web sales sites in order to sell yourself to a company specializing in cyberspace.

Whatever the case, the first place to start is—you guessed it four-eyes—the library. If you're not a regular library user, go to your nearest reference desk, be sweet as pie, and put your queries into the hands of a professional. They won't do the search for you, but they'll show you where to go. To begin, ask for a catalogue called *Scott's Directories*, which is put out by the Southam Information and Technology Group. *Scott's* lists every industry you can think of wanting to work for, with a specific book for Ontario, Quebec, the Maritimes, the western provinces, and Toronto and surrounding area.

You look up each subject by its code, a list of which is carried at the back of the book. Under each heading there's a list of all the companies in the area that deal in that particular industry. And all for the low, low price of nothing because that's what's cool about the library. It's free. The list of companies includes phone numbers, addresses, and contact names. Read up on cold calling though (Chapter 5) before you approach them.

Another key source (did I tell you this section was loaded or what?) is *The Canadian Almanac and Directory*, which is published each year. This book is a gold mine of information, covering every federal, provincial, and municipal government office as well as all Canadian television stations, exhibitions, hospitals, book publishers, law offices, and the Canadian Sheep Breeders Association in Red Deer, Alberta. That doesn't come close to touching on the categories this book covers. It even gives contact names for many of the companies, which comes in handy for cold calls and cover letters. This book is so amazing I can't even begin to describe how wonderful it is. Just go look it up.

If you want more information about a particular "big player" company (a company that generates a lot of income) you can look the name up in Dun and Bradstreet Canada's *Canadian Key Business Directory*. It lists the businesses that are in the top three percent or do twenty million dollars a year in sales or have 100 or more total employees or have a million-dollar net worth or have branches with more than 500 employees. This information allows you to determine which of your target companies is big or expanding—knowledge you can tailor into specific interview material. For instance, if a company's on the list it would not be good to tell an interviewer that you prefer small companies, like to work independently, and think that all corporate Canadians are greedy, money-hungry pigs.

Another great source is the *Canada Student Employment Guide*, which is published each year by the Student Employment Network and written by a cool guy named Kevin Makra. He contacted over 300 companies in Canada and got the low-down on what you need to start working there full time. At the end of each entry, he adds some information on summer and part-time work, so it's definitely worth a look for those of you who still have some years of school to go.

Another source you could try is *The Career Directory* (Edcore Publishing Corp.). This book is geared for full-time job hunters, but Section 4 contains a Summer Job Index that can be used by those of you who want jobs leading to a businessy type of career. The Summer Job Index lists companies that hire summer students, and readers should use this Index in conjunction with the Education Index earlier in the book.

Don't forget what my high school librarian always called "periodicals," but what I like to call magazines and newspapers. Once again, put yourself in the angelic hands of your local librarian book goddess (or god) and find the *Canadian Index*, formerly known as the *Canadian Business Index*, published by Micro Media Limited. It has both a subject index, a corporate name index, and a personal index. These indexes contain the headlines of any articles that have been published in Canada about a specific company or a specific employee. Use this book to research a company by scanning the headlines and then reading the full articles from the periodicals section (ask your saintly librarian to help you find the articles if necessary).

Researching a company puts you more on the level with an employer, who'll be impressed by your interest and understanding of company business. When I applied for a job at my video store, one of the things I knew a lot about was other video stores. I also had an idea of what was happening with that particular chain—that it was trying to compete with big chain stores, and that more stores were opening soon. All this information came up in the interview, including every video store I belong to (scarily, there are about seven or eight). The manager and I exchanged opinions on particular stores, locations, and stock. Know your stuff, even for the most banal-seeming of jobs. Employers want to know that you didn't just wander in off the street—you came looking for their store in particular.

Research can also take place when you ask people who are "in the know" what they think. Say you heard about a summer job at a golf club pro shop. What would be some of ways you could research that job without ever going near a library? Two things pop to mind. First, you could ask people you know who play golf what they use a pro shop for, what kind of service they like, and what their favourite products are. Second, you could go into a sports store that carries golf equipment and check out their display. Get familiar with the name brands and then cosy up to a salesperson and ask their opinion of the stuff. Now when you walk into the interview, you know more than just how to ring up a purchase. You're already familiar with the equipment and the customer base. Whether the interviewer recognizes the depth of your research or not, you'll feel the difference.

## Checking Out the Net

Okay, surfers and techies, I'm not going to pretend to be Ms. Cool Cybertech Chick with a name like Crash Override. I'm barely on top of my little home computer. So I'm not going to profess to tell you how to best surf the Net for jobs. Instead, I'm going to mention that there's a lot of job information and résumé posting on the Internet. Further, there are ways to use your computer to help you get a job. In order to learn about this, if you're interested, I suggest you pick up the book *Get Wired, You're Hired*, by Mark Swartz. He's way cooler than I am about this stuff, and his book will have all the updated sites that you need. In the meantime, there are lots of newspaper articles you could dig up about this new wave of job hiring.

Here are some places to start. Some can be way too "adult" oriented, but you may find directions to specific student stuff.

Addresses for connections to other sites:

> Canadian Job Source
> http://www.irus.rri.uwo.ca/%7Ejlaw/job_can.html

Produced by a graduate student at Queen's University, this site contains a huge list of Canadian-related sites.

> CanWorkNet
> http://www.canworknet.ca/cwn/english/main.html

A joint project of Human Resources Development and the private sector. Sorted by province.

> The Parksville/Qualicum Career Centre home page
> http://qb.island.net/~careers/cc/canjob.html

Sponsored by the B.C. employment ministry, this site gives concise descriptions (and lots of links) to Canadian job/career sites. A good place to start.

Other interesting sites:

> The Monster Board
> http://www.monster.com

Owned by Cala Recruiting of Montreal, this is a virtual career centre. Originally built by a U.S. company, much of the material is geared for the American market. Check out their "Roar" pages for students.

> Human Resources Development Canada's home page
> http://hrdc-drhc.gc.ca

Offers a variety of info about government programs. A good way to avoid being put on hold for the same information.

> Student Employment Network
> www.studentjobs.com

Kevin Makra's Web site, which is based on his book *The Canada Student Employment Guide.*

And now the time has come my friends to get out of your house, out of the library, and out of the Dairy Queen ("please, please just one more Oreo Fudge Brownie Blizzard before I have to talk to strangers on the phone . . ."), and make contact with people who are going to get you working.

CHAPTER 5

# True Urban Tales of Job Hunting

So you've got the résumé. You've got the cover letter. You know your skills because you've been articulating them to the dog for the last seven days straight. Now you've got to leave the house.

So how do you go about *actually* getting a job? Here are the methods that most students use:

- Contacts
- Cold Calls
- Newspapers
- Employment Centres
- Pounding the Pavement

Okay. Great. Chapter's done. Off you go.

Oh how nice, you're still here . . . but I'll bet you're looking at that painfully obvious how-to-get-a-job list, thinking "I knew that already!" So smart cookie, whatcha reading this for? Let's face it, none of us like doing the icky stuff between deciding we need a job and saying "I'll take it." What this chapter aims to do is not to tell you the obvious, but to inspire you to head out for that great summer job about which you've been dreaming all these cold winter nights.

Let's all admit it. It's hard. Even the most seasoned pros find that their knees quake or their stomachs quiver at the thought of approaching someone for a job. Okay, so some store manager has more power at this juncture than you do. So some measly government official is going to be the one to put the stamp of approval on your application. So some know-it-all friend of your parents is the key to the job you want. So what. Keep your eye on the greater purpose. You're out there to learn, to get some experience, to make some money. None of these people owns your soul, and when the summer ends you might even have acquired an appreciation for school, fleeting as that may be.

In our society we invest so much of our identity in the jobs we do. This is a great time to realize that being able to scoop ice cream efficiently or stack creamed corn properly doesn't have a whole hell of a lot to do with who you are. So bite the bullet, get out there, and give it a shot. Whatever you're going for, there are other jobs and other people who'll hire you, so don't get discouraged if the one you wanted doesn't work out. You never know who's just around the corner with a hiring sign.

Now I'm going to take you through each of the ways you actually go out and get a job. Each method is slightly different in its approach, and each is best designed for certain types of jobs. So if you know what you're doing, pick up the phone, pick up a paper, or pick up the pace of your résumé distribution. But if you need a little motivation and encouragement, read on.

## Contacts, or Getting a Helping Hand from the Family

For any job search you do, this is the logical place to start. If you want to be a painter and your older sister owns a painting company, why would you try to get hired somewhere else? Unless your sister is a veritable sociopath, in which case I understand, going with who you know is the easiest and most sensible of all ways to get a job. Most jobs of any kind are obtained this way. Adults are incredibly understanding about the difficulties and hardships of job-getting, and most of the time they want to help. Almost a hundred percent of the students I interviewed had gotten at least one job with the help of their parents. These students often seemed embarrassed when they told me their parents had hired them, but I say more power to you if that's how you get the job. It's not shameful, it's sensible. Contact jobs are about gaining valuable experience for your résumé with less stress and strife. That's called common sense.

Also helpful are friends of your parents and parents of your friends. Once you get going, the list is endless. The number one important step is to get the word out that you're looking for a summer job. No one can help you if you keep this needing a job thing a secret. And the more specific you can be the better. Once people know what you're looking for, they'll know if they can help you. Then Uncle Bob can say "Oh, I know someone at the HMV store downtown. I'll call him up for you." Those are the magic contact words. The next best thing is having someone like your friend Larry's dad say "Call up that autobody shop and tell them Big Lar sent ya." It's better if he calls them first, but the next best thing is having a name to get you in the door. Now you're networking.

Even if the HMV or the autobody shop isn't hiring, they might have another idea for who to call or where to go. You use your last contact to get your next contact. And you're no longer just some jobless no-name off the street, 'cause "Big Lar sent ya."

## Mindless Robot Syndrome

I know so many people who've gone through this scenario. Mom says, "I talked to Al Hackman the other day about you needing a job and he's agreed to see you. Phone and make an appointment." At these words, the thinking, breathing, intelligent you turns off and a robot takes over your brain. "Phone Al. Get job" repeats over and over in what used to be your left temporal lobe. You walk into Al's office, having thought through nothing, and when the great contact leans over the desk and says "What do you want me to do for you?" the real you wakes up and realizes that you haven't the faintest clue what Al Hackman does for a living, much less what you want to do for the summer.

I and others I know have been caught by the promise of a connection. We make the mistake of thinking Contact From Parent = Job. On occasion it does. But you'll have a much greater chance of scoring a job off a contact if you know a) what they do and the scope of their ability to help you, b) what you want to do for the summer other than "get hired" (see Chapter 1), and c) what would be most helpful to you—a phone call, some advice, a reference, an interview. Never assume that they can actually get you a job unless they offer. If you're clear, articulate, and give them a good résumé to go by, they'll have an easier time selling you to whomever they think might hire you. You've got to help them out by reassuring them that they're not vouching for an idiot (particularly if they've never met you before).

Once you've been promised the goods by a well-placed contact, don't start spending those pay cheques until the job is truly in hand. It's always good to keep several possibilities going at once, and see what pans out. Which leads me to:

## The Tale of Artistic Differences

Martha, as you might remember from Chapter 1, is my roommate and fellow writer. She didn't always want to be a writer; in fact at one point she wanted to go into the fast-paced, big-bucks world of theatre. Martha envisioned herself as both a scenic designer and a director. Now although she has talents in these areas, she had no training whatsoever except for two measly credit courses at university and three plays. No matter, Martha was convinced that it was only a matter of weeks before she'd take the theatre world by storm.

She began networking for a summer job at a garden party of her father's business associates. Floating through the crowd in her party dress, mingling and chatting with the guests Martha gracefully indicated her wish to work in theatre for the summer. The party-goers were extremely supportive, waving over one older gentleman who said he'd help her. "I'm on the Board of Directors of the Maple Leaf Theatre Company, and I'll get you a job." So easy! Martha was ecstatic.

On the day of her interview she put on her power suit (an orange linen number that made her look like a power pumpkin), put her portfolio under her arm, and marched down to the theatre—where she was left waiting . . . and waiting. Finally, in crept a harried-looking man who identified himself as the artistic director. He was dressed in ratty jeans and a T-shirt, with bad hair and an awkward, condescending manner. Martha reached out a confident hand, knowing that the job was already in the bag . . . when he asked, "What's your name again?"

Martha couldn't believe it. This guy had no idea who her contact was, much less who she was. He continued, "I don't know how you got an appointment. We don't need anybody. The director's already got two interns and the shows pretty much hire their own people." Apparently Mr. Board of Directors was a little underinformed when it came to the hiring processes of his company. Unfortunately Martha got caught in the middle of both unknowing parties.

"You can't imagine," she told me, "how embarrassing it was to be told by this LOSER that I couldn't work there. He even went on to say that no one he'd ever heard of had been both a director and a scenic designer. I had planned my life out already, and here was this guy who looked like he couldn't paint his way out of a paper bag telling me that my dream of doing both jobs was impossible." The happy ending? Martha went to New Hampshire and worked for peanuts doing set design and directing, nearly killing herself in the process and ridding herself of the need to ever do that again. But she did it. Now she's nixed theatre entirely, instead aiming for the fast-paced, big-bucks world of film.

The moral of this story is that networking will open a lot of doors, but just because you made it into the foyer doesn't mean you're getting past the concierge.

On the other hand, one student I know had a contact who'd just got a job running municipal utilities in a relatively big city. His big-shot contact had just passed along his résumé, thinking it would be considered along with the rest. His underlings, however, regarded this act as the ultimatum from the chief to take our student on. They called our guy up to tell him, "We have no job for you to do, but you start work Monday." Through a fortuitous networking misunderstanding he got full-time employment picking pennies out of fountains and spraying walks covered with goose droppings. So contacts might work in your favour as well.

A note of caution: as awesome as it is to get a job because somebody high up made a quick phone call, sometimes there can be a few repercussions in the job itself. Some students report that other staff treat them differently when they know the orders came from a bigwig at the company. You might have even slid your way into someone else's shifts because no one had anticipated hiring you, which won't warm the other employees' hearts to your presence either. Thems the breaks folks. Hopefully, whatever tension you encounter will be lessened by the fact that you're there to do a good job too. And if you can keep your way in quiet I suggest you do, since it'll sustain the illusion of equality. Otherwise grin and bear it, 'cause at least you've got a job.

## Contact Phone Calls-- Getting Warmer

We'll go into more depth about cold calls momentarily. A contact call is a bit different, hence those of us in the business wittily call it a "warm" call. This is when the person you're calling is expecting to hear from you, or at least knows who you are and who you've talked to. Therefore you don't have to brazen your way in; you can simply identify yourself as Big Lar's nephew, and that alone will get the attention of the person you're calling.

## Calling All Contacts

1. Remember to first identify yourself and then the person who recommended your call. That's the secret password that'll get you in the door. "My name is Matthew Flufftree—my mother, Susan Flufftree, spoke to your husband, and he directed me to you."
2. If you get the receptionist or assistant, give them the essential contact name as well as your own. Always be polite and helpful to the assistant! They hold the power of getting your message delivered. Another option is to ask if the person has voice mail. That way you can leave a more detailed message and the person will listen to it directly, rather than receive a piece of paper with your name on it.
3. Be clear about your objective. This goes for both assistants and the person you want to talk to. It's key to remember that the more they know about what

you want to do, the better they can help you. You'll find that they'll get frustrated if they don't know what you want.

4. When you speak to a contact on the phone, request just twenty minutes of their time in a scheduled appointment so that you can ask for their advice. Most likely a contact will help you get a job if it's in their power to do so. Otherwise, they may have valuable advice on who you could approach. The contact may just want to give you the information on the phone, which is also okay.

5. Write any names down! Get their numbers if your contact has them. Make sure you understand their titles and what they do. Do they own the video store, manage the video store, or just work there and know the manager? You'll be approaching these people, so go armed with as much information as possible.

6. If the contact doesn't say so already, ask if you can use his or her name when approaching these other people. You need permission to use the new password. Bonus points if the contact makes a call for you, either to set up an appointment or to get you in touch with someone new.

7. Always remember to send thank-you notes to people who've helped you (see Chapter 4 on how to write one). Not only will this send Miss Manners and your mother into joyous frenzies of celebration, but since you never know when these people might help you again it's both savvy and considerate to appreciate them. If someone's contact pans out into a job, write another thank-you letter or phone to let them know they helped. People love to hear that they've contributed, and it puts them in a good frame of mind about you. Not a lot of people send thank-you notes, so they can make you stand out.

Finally, take people seriously when they offer to help you. If someone suggests that they could help, ask if it's all right to call them at work the next day. A friend of mine whose father is in the food business once suggested casually that I could get a job working in her dad's office that summer. I was afraid to push the point because I didn't want to seem, well, pushy, so I let it slide for three weeks while I tried to get a job through a variety of unsuccessful methods. One day I said tiredly, "I hate looking for a job!" I was just venting, but my friend looked at me incredulously and said "I told you I'd get you a job." The next day I was signed up to work at her dad's office. Some people might back down from their offer to help, but that has nothing to do with you. Most people are sincere in their efforts to assist you. Accept it.

## Generating Contacts

If you're feeling trapped because you know absolutely no one in the area you wish to pursue, you'll have to do extra work to enter the field. It's not fair, but there it is. If you're really dedicated to getting a job in a particular company or field, it's still possible despite your lack of contacts. How? You generate them yourself.

By generate I mean that you create contacts out of your persistence, passion, and creativity. A good example is a student named Josh who I spoke to about photography. Now photography is a difficult field to break into, and even more so if you're still a student. But Josh really loved cameras. He spent a lot of time fiddling around with them, learning the basics, and taking whatever pictures he could, and whenever. Josh took photo courses, and made a friend at a photo store who from time to time would let him borrow professional equipment just to try it out. One summer Josh was working in another capacity in a big-name clothes store, and a well-known band came in to do a photo shoot with the clothing. Josh persuaded his boss that the store could save money if he did it, since he knew how to use the equipment. Not only did he save the company thousands of dollars, he shot great work.

When he went to university Josh took his portfolio to Campus Relations and became their only student photographer. Through this work he hooked up with professional photojournalists from the local paper, and developed such a close rapport with them that they persuaded their boss to create an internship so that Josh could work at the paper after school. In the meantime, the clothing store hired him back during the summers and he did their catalogue, saving them yet more money. Back at school, other universities in the area were calling him to do work for them. One day he got a call from the U.S. Democratic Party, asking him to be one of two photographers to take pictures of Jesse Jackson when he came into town to speak.

Josh's incredible story goes on, and will go on as he further explores the area he loves. My point is that when he started Josh had little connection to the world of photojournalism, but his interest in the subject, his enthusiasm for learning, and his willingness to take a chance helped him to create his own contacts.

The same thing can happen for you if you want the job badly enough. It may take time, but don't ever limit your dreams because you think you can't be someone who's "connected." Besides, you never know what connections your neighbour or someone beside you on the bus has. Strike up conversations and articulate your interests. That's the only way things can happen—when other people know about it.

# Cold Calls, or Telephone Tag with Strangers

Colds calls have to be one of the single most frightening chores on earth. Many people would take lead-weight parachuting over having to pick up the phone and chat to someone they don't know. Well, you're in luck. I just happen to be an expert in making cold calls, and I'm going to make it as easy as possible for you.

First of all, what is a cold call and where does it work? A cold call is made to a person who's not expecting to hear from you and doesn't know who you are. That's what makes these suckers so difficult; you're already nervous about asking "Can you help me?" and to make things worse the person on the other end has absolutely no compelling reason to listen to you except out of the goodness of their hearts.

But in fact you do have something compelling to offer—you. You're not calling to ask for spare change, you're calling to offer your services in exchange for a pay cheque. And don't undervalue those services, because this world wouldn't run without students like us to man the coffee shops, clothes stores, and lawn mowers. So although you feel yourself to be in the underdog position, know that somewhere out there someone's having a terrible day because their busboy just quit and two waiters called in sick and they need you!

I too faced these fears. In the past, cold calls were something I did almost trance-like—I'd get out my piece of paper with the number and the name of the person I was calling. I'd prepare my opening gambit, and then, regardless of whether the person answering said yes or no to my request, I'd hang up feeling more anxious than when I started. Over time I've learned a couple of things that really help.

## 1. Preparation

This seems like such a simple concept, but most of the time we just want to get the call over with so badly that we're punching in the phone number before we've thought past the word "hello." Preparation is the ticket to interview express. At this point you want to answer for yourself the questions "Who am I?" "What have I done?" and "What do I want?"

Read the following examples. Notice how each person takes the time to clearly introduce themselves, give a specific place where they did some applicable work, and then articulate what they're looking for.

| | |
|---|---|
| Who am I? | Hi, my name is Dan Wong, and I'm a student at Fairview Public School. |
| What have I done? | This past summer and this spring I helped to repair my family's cabin. I learned how to do roofing, tarring, painting, and some electrical work. The cabin is now in working condition and winterized. |
| What do I want? | I'm looking for a construction job at any level where I can work regular hours for the summer. |

| | |
|---|---|
| Who am I? | Hello, my name is Sonu Noria. |
| What have I done? | At my school, I co-organized the spring carnation drive for charity. We raised $500, the highest amount ever for this event. I also volunteer every other week at the Golden Eves Seniors Home, where I read and talk to the residents. |
| What do I want? | I was wondering if you have a student position this summer at your Foundation, in which I could both work with cancer patients and also help in the office. |

| | |
|---|---|
| Who am I? | Hello, my name is Quinn Vorster, I was directed to you by camp director Bruce Harris. |
| What have I done? | I spent part of the spring term teaching grade seven and eight kids how to play tennis, as well as coaching the junior team. I also played in the city finals representing the senior team. |
| What do I want? | I'm looking to teach tennis this summer to all ages and levels, using both drills and fun games. Could you tell me about your sports program, particularly tennis? |

Notice that if you put your hand over the left column, the right column becomes a perfect opening statement to use when cold-calling employers.

Thinking out this part of the phone call is crucial. Most people call up employers and ask for a job without taking the time to either introduce themselves or give any reason why the person on the other end would be interested. Your little introductory dialogue should take no more than thirty seconds. Once you've finished, the person on the other end has a good idea of what you're about and what you're looking for. This translates into a very professional beginning to your conversation and eliminates some of the underdog "please don't kick me when I'm down" feeling.

Don't hesitate to practise that introduction out loud. Once you know it really well, you'll be comfortable with what you're saying and that'll be apparent in the way you say it. You want to speak freely and easily, not stiffly. Tape yourself, or get someone else to rehearse with you.

This is the approach I alluded to in the first chapter that helped me get a camp job teaching drama. I was very clear about the kind of camp I wanted (co-ed, all ages, mix of activities, medium-sized), and I was very clear about what I wanted to do. As a result, the camp directors I spoke to were respectful of my preference because I already sounded like an expert, and they were all to the point about whether or not they could help me. One man told me his camp only did puppet shows. Another woman liked my credentials but had already filled the position, and so asked me to send my CV for next year. Another director informed me that there was only the position of piano player left (which, unless the camp wanted their musical number to be the easy, one-handed version of "Chariots of Fire," was probably not for me). Within eight phone calls I hit the camp that had the program I was looking for—and the spot was still available.

## 2. Technological Preparation

Often when you're cold calling someone to propose an idea or to offer your services there may be reason to fax your possible employer something. Many jobs already ask you to fax your résumé rather than mail or hand deliver it. It's very savvy and impressive to have already prepared a résumé and cover letter, and even a proposal if it applies, and then offer to send it immediately if the person you speak to sounds interested. If you don't have a fax at home, find out where the closest fax service is—whether it's the post office or the printing shop—so that you can make a dash once the résumé request has been made.

Another little tip is to use the cover sheet of the fax to write a more personal message. A sentence or two directed at the person receiving the fax—with a reference to any previous interaction you've had and an appreciation of the time they're taking to look at your résumé—will make you seem more human in the face of fax paper.

After you send the fax, call to make sure that the person got it and that it's legible. This also makes for an excellent chance to befriend someone, for example the person's assistant, on the other end of the phone. Interest in the state of your résumé translates as interest in getting the job. That alone may catapult you into the "yes" pile.

## 3. Negotiating Voice Mail

I used to hate getting someone's voice mail, and so I'd hang up whenever I heard it click into "You've reached Blah Blah on Wednesday July 14th . . . ." What I've since discovered is the advantage of voice mail over leaving a message with a receptionist or assistant. Voice mail is like your own private little sell-yourself spot, wherein you can leave your full prepared message without having to negotiate for someone's time. The best results come from clearly stating who you are and what you want in a friendly way, and letting them know that if you don't hear from them in three days to a week, you'll call again. The amazing thing about voice mail is that by the time you actualy talk to the person you're already familiar to him or her, so it feels less like a cold call. Honest to god, I've made friends with people before I've ever spoken to them directly. Take a deep breath before you leave the message (during the beep) and then put all your enthusiasm into it. If you're stiff with phones and messages, practise them first. When you're actually leaving the message, make yourself smile—you can change the tone of your voice that way. Try it the next time you're feeling impatient with someone on the other end of the phone.

## 4. Be Patient

When you leave a message for someone you have to understand that you're probably last on their list of daily priorities, especially if they don't know you. They're going to take their time calling you back. Even contact-oriented phone calls are often slow to be returned. This isn't an insult, it's a reality. You're sitting at home waiting for them to call you. They're in an office with three presentations, ten screw-ups by the regional guys, and a broken computer—all to be dealt with by the end of the day. Take heart and be patient.

## 5. Ask Questions without a Job Agenda

More often than not, when students (or anyone) are cold calling for a job their overwhelming concern is for themselves. This is a perfectly natural reaction. But what it means is that cold callers usually get stuck when they ask the question "Are you hiring?" because when they get no for an answer they give up. Consider a cold call as more than just a request for a job. You can use it to ask for advice or information, or to find out what the company is looking for in young people.

You have to understand the essential truth here. People love to talk about their jobs. Honestly. It's because we rarely ask anything about a person's job beyond "What do you do?", and even that's usually a dinner party conversation tool not meant for in-depth analysis. People love love love to explain to other people about their jobs—the ins and outs, the trials, the rewards. People also love to give advice. Advice-giving is a sign of superiority, and confers on both parties the honour of respect. So ask questions. And ask them genuinely, for the sake of knowing about a job you might want to do, hiring contract or no.

For this book I interviewed a DJ from a big Toronto nightclub. I didn't want to disturb him for more than ten minutes; I just wanted some essential information. Well, he got so excited, he talked for an hour. And then he phoned me back because there was something he forgot. I could have written ten pages on being a DJ when he was done. Further, he invited me to come to his club anytime. So not only am I completely well-versed on the ins and outs of being a DJ, I can get on the guest list whenever I want. That wasn't the intention of my phone call, but when you make a genuine connection with someone the possibilities are limitless.

## 6. Be Persistent

One student offered some great advice. Michelle's method was to call specific people more than once, asking them questions about the company or business and in the process building a rapport with them. For instance, she was trying to get a job as a nanny but the agency wouldn't hire her because they thought she was too young. Michelle hung in there and developed a phone relationship with the hiring office. She was personable and consistent, but not a nuisance. The employers finally had her come in for an interview, and to their surprise they found themselves hiring her because she convinced them that she could do the job. Michelle used this method a few years later with the Nike footwear company. Instead of going through Human Resources, she began talking to other people in the specific department she wanted to work in. She asked them about the company and what kind of experience they thought she needed to work there. At the time there weren't any jobs available and she knew that, but within a month or two a job came up, they phoned her, and she got it. Finding ways to understand the company and the people who worked there paid off.

Another student told me that one summer he picked up the phone book, contacted every construction company listed, and asked for a job. He didn't have much experience, but he hit a foreman who'd just fired someone and needed a replacement worker immediately. You never know when you might call just at the moment they're short someone and need you.

## Newspapers, or the Column at the Back of the Classifieds

Another possibility is the newspaper. Flip to the classifieds that you always ignore when you're looking for horoscopes, Ann Landers, sports scores, or the comics. You'll know it because of all the little tiny columns. Look for the heading that has to do with Students—Summer Work. (Sometimes known as Seasonal Work.) Look down that column. With pen circle possible jobs.

Yes, that's pretty much how Using-The-Newspaper-To-Get-A-Job works. Of course, then you have to call and make an appointment, which is essentially a cold call. The thing to remember with the paper is that the summer job of your dreams is rarely advertised there. Most of the ads are placed by telemarketing firms, door-to-door sales outfits, warehouses, and places that need to recruit a mass of people. However, I once got a decent lifeguarding job through the classifieds, since the advertiser was a pool company hiring for all their individual pools that summer and needed a mass of employees.

The pitfalls of the newspaper are those crappy jobs that get advertised in the student column. You can usually spot them because they sound like great deals.

NO EXPERIENCE NECESSARY
WE TRAIN YOU
STUDENTS WELCOME
INCLUDES BONUSES

Some or all of these phrases may be included in the pitch. They want students who feel they have no other options this summer, because they aren't aware of their skills and experiences like you are. Another tip-off is if the ad repeats day after day, week after week. If the ad is still there a month or two later, BEWARE. The turnover is high, either because the job sucks or they fire everyone to save themselves money through tax loopholes.

## Employment Centres, or the One-Stop Job Shop

When I think of employment centres, I think of those Depression-era pictures of sad-looking men hanging around waiting for a job posting to be announced and then knocking the guy down beside them to get at that 60 cents a day job. Not a particularly positive connection. Luckily for you, the current federal youth employment centres, now called Human Resource Development Centres, are much more friendly and positive places.

Now I don't want you to panic, but I'm about to give you information that sounds really serious and like something you'd read in your guidance office at school, but if you skim through this section you might find out something important and then afterwards I'll tell you a good story and it'll all be okay.

## Federal Employment Centres

There are over 300 Canada Employment Centres for Students across Canada (called Hire-A-Student in Alberta and Student Youth Employment Centres in Manitoba). These are federally funded youth employment centres that open in late April and May to help students get summer jobs. One of the ways they do this is by providing incentives to employers to hire students with their Summer Job Action Program. In their Summer Career Placement program, they provide wage incentives to organizations that can offer career-related jobs for the summer. More to the point, they also encourage these and other employers to advertise on their job boards, creating an excellent way to find out what specific jobs are out there this coming summer.

Each of the individual Canada Employment Centres for Students (CECS) tailor their programs and literature to what jobs the region supplies and the students have shown interest in. Even more promising, the Summer Employment Officers (SEOs) are full-time university and college students. This means that instead of a bored, overworked, impatient government counsellor, you can get guidance and advice from someone who isn't so far out of the process that the last summer job they remember was in the good ol' days of '42.

The centres offer Group Information sessions on everything from résumés to networking to interview skills. Since a book is only one way to learn, I encourage you to take advantage of any skills training you can get, particularly for free. The SEOs also provide one-on-one counselling and résumé help. If you have trouble with typing, they just might be kind enough to help you there too. You can get your résumé looked over by experts and laser printed too. Who said the government was all bad?

Of course you'll also want to check out the job boards at the centres. They're typically divided into job types, and you and a bunch of other lost souls will wander around the board with pencil and paper looking for jobs that sound promising or at least within your skill range. Remember to write down all the information they give you, as you never know what will be relevant.

One warning, which was echoed by the head of the Ontario CECS: don't think these are the only jobs out there. They most definitely aren't. The employment centres are one source out of many. Take responsibility and go out there looking for yourself. For one thing, you'll be competing with a lot fewer people if you're out on your own. For another, it keeps you from pinning your summer hopes and dreams on the Canadian government.

The aim of these centres is to get students hired. If your aim is to get hired this summer, they're worth a visit.

## Maximizing Your Use of the Employment Centre

Having hung out in one of these employment centres, quietly observing and interviewing student counsellors, I can tell you for sure that there are good ways and bad ways to approach your use of the centre. For instance, it's good to bring your résumé because sometimes the centre will have five spots open for one job interview and the first five résumés they receive will get the spots. It's bad to bring your mother to the centre (and don't think mothers don't come), since you might as well figure it out on your own and she probably won't be allowed to come to any interviews you might get. It's good to go early in the season, go often (every two days keeps you on track of new postings), and arrive before noon when new job postings go up. It's bad to show up, register for a program, and then never call back to actually get the work.

If you're looking for your first job, these centres could be your sanity-saving pit stop. First, they're always posting mass hirings for special events, wherein you can get quick cash, quick work experience, and a reference for something as innocuous as "table clearer" or "food hawker." Further, the centres will sometimes offer day programs, like a park clean-up, for which you'll get a certificate, a reference, and a free lunch. And what's more, if you're worried about references, making yourself known to employment counsellors on a regular basis will probably result in one of them offering to vouch for you.

As for the job boards, take your time to assess the information that each posting offers. Write it all down—here's an idea, bring your own notebook so that you don't lose the little pieces of scrap paper everyone else uses—and double-check phone numbers and addresses. Once you've got some possibilities, check with the counsellors to see if they have any more information on the job. Then go home, or to a quiet place, prepare your approach (see the Cold Calls section of this chapter), and begin your search. Don't cram yourself into a phone booth a block away from the centre to make your calls unless you're absolutely sure that you're just booking an appointment.

Phew! You made it! Now the story I promised you.

## The Tale of the Extra-Value Employees

One of the things the youth employment counsellors always tell their jobless charges, and rightly so, is to research the companies they apply to. As we've already discussed, researching a company gives you some information to relate to, and will impress even the most jaded employer.

One summer not too long ago, two fifteen-year-old guys were looking for their first jobs. Not only were they hampered by the usual woes of inexperience, but Tran, who was from Vietnam, and Raji, who was from Pakistan, were finding that their current level of English was creating a bit of a barrier to most jobs. They were at the centre every day, but they were having no luck getting work.

Feeling disheartened by the whole process, they opened up to their regular employment counsellor down at the centre, and confessed to him that their real dream was to work at McDonald's. "We gotta work at McDonald's," they pleaded, and our counsellor knew these two needed an edge. He explained to them that researching the company would show their enthusiasm and knowledge blah blah blah, just as I've already explained to you. He watched them leave, feeling that it was hoping too much to see them get their dream jobs.

I guess he underestimated the strength of his own advice. These two aspiring employees went to the local McDonald's and spent the afternoon memorizing the entire menu: food, beverages, prices, and all. The day of their interview dawned and they went through the usual application process. Finally, at the very end of the interview, the manager asked them if they had any special skills to add to the job. Tran looked at Raji and Raji looked at Tran and then the two of them in stereo began reciting the menu. They listed everything, in order, to the flabbergasted employer, and didn't stop until they had described each and every item, right down to the Extra Value meals.

As a result, their dream came true and they became members of the McDonald's team. Of course the first day on the job Tran burned the chicken black. But that's another book.

## Pounding the Pavement, or These Nikes Are Made for Walkin'

Speaking of taking responsibility for your own job hunting, don't forget that there's always the option of simply heading out there, résumés in hand, to find the job in person. This means both cruising for Help Wanted signs in store windows and biting the bullet by going into a place that may not be hiring but asking anyway on the off chance that they are.

No joke, this is a brutal method of instant rejection. On the other hand, both my roommate and I support our writing careers with jobs that we got walking in off the street. It takes confidence to enter a strange store, ask for the manager, and try to sell that person on why he or she needs you. But let me re-frame this for you. Eventually, the odds are that you'll walk into some place that actually does need someone to fill in. As I mentioned with cold calls, you never know when someone will get sick, quit, get fired, or plan to open a new store. You've just got to be there when it happens.

There are several key elements to the walking-in-off-the-street approach that will help you immensely.

## 1. Be (or Appear to Be) Confident

It's amazing how draining it is to put yourself in a vulnerable position by walking into strange stores several times a day. You start strong and then your drive starts to waver, and you begin assessing stores from the outside and deciding they look pretty much fully employed, and so you begin skipping stores until you see what may be a friendly person, so you go in and they say no and then you don't feel like working with anyone who isn't friendly, or in any place that has brown art on the walls or sells crafts, so you just skip a few stores, and you start mumbling at the managers, turning to leave the moment they say no. . . .

Yes, it sucks. And your powers of rationalization will convince you that at this point it would be a way better idea to stop for a milkshake or go watch Oprah rather than try another store today. You must overcome the sensible part of your mind, which is screaming "Avoid rejection, avoid rejection!" and convince yourself that your personal worth is not invested in whether or not some store manager tells you they're hiring. Once you've determined that your ego isn't involved, you can detach that part of your brain, and cheerily approach store managers with a big smile and the confidence that not only do they have the power to help you, but that you have the power to help them . . . if they have shifts available.

If you don't feel confident, walk into that store AS IF you were a confident person. What do I mean by "as if"? Think about this: if you're walking across your garden and you see a bit of the garden hose and you think for a second that it's a snake, what do you do? Do you go turn the snake on? No, you jump sideways and hope it won't get you, and THEN when you realize that it's actually the garden hose, you hope like hell that no one saw you jump at a little piece of green rubber tubing. The point is, no matter what you thought you saw, you behaved "as if" it were a snake and it didn't make a difference what it *actually* was.

So let's apply this to you. If you're really nervous, but you act as if you're not, who's to know the difference except you? So think, how does a confident person act? A confident person walks tall, looks people in the eye, feels like they have a right to be there, and asserts that by not slouching in the corner. Pick someone you think of as really confident (and I bet if you asked them they'd admit to feeling unconfident at least some of the time) and pretend you're that person for the day. Don't walk into a store, stride in and go for it.

## 2. Get Your Timing and Your Entrance Down

Any movie star who's ever gone to the Oscars could tell you that timing and attitude are the keys to success. I know a restaurant manager as sweet as pie who'll throw out any résumé she gets between 11 a.m. and 2 p.m. Why? It irritates her that the applicant hasn't thought about the fact that that's the busiest time for a restaurant, and so she figures they don't understand the food service industry (not to mention that they've bothered her at her biggest stress point of the day). Think ahead. Don't try to apply to a video store on a weekend (biggest rental time) or a Monday (largest amount of returns). Don't apply to a restaurant during peak hours. Most retail stores, banks, and food places get a rush of customers over the lunch hour when office people can run errands. This isn't the time to try to connect with the manager and make an impression, because these people are going to be stressed. Think ahead. Go earlier (or later, during the lull after 2:30 but well before 5). Do a reconnaissance mission at the stores of your choice. What's the quietest time in the store? Who's in charge of the store? Who's *really* in charge of the store? What days does the nice manager work?

Our restaurant manager also told me that she hates people who Rollerblade into her store. Try to look as though you want to be there, and that you're not just passing through on your 77th résumé drop. We'll get into clothing later, but present yourself in a similar (not exact, similar) standard of dress as the employees. Make an effort to connect to that particular store or restaurant. Look like you belong.

## 3. Bring a Résumé and a Personalized Cover Letter

Another way you can get noticed is to bring a résumé and a good cover letter (see Chapters 2 and 3) that's personalized for that particular store or job. If the letter is engaging enough, you're more likely to get a response than if you just leave an application like everyone else. We've gone over the power of good résumés and cover letters. No more need be said.

## 4. Fill Out Requisite Forms

Often the big chain stores will have standardized employment application forms. You want to find out whether these forms exist, because if you just leave a résumé they could throw it out if it doesn't cover the exact information they ask for. If you're applying to this type of place, one tip is to list your available hours on your résumé. Shift jobs require people to fill hours and often the key to a job is being available when other people aren't. Letting them know that you're very very available may be the thing that gets their attention. Try to be as flexible as possible about your hours.

## 5. Pay Attention to Expanding Stores

Another thing to watch for is whether a store is expanding in size, hours, or opening at another location. This is a good time to offer your services, as they may be eager for people to fill empty shifts. Be quick about it though. Big stores often have a combination of imported people from other stores plus some new hirees. Don't wait when you see that HIRING sign; you need to make your impact soon because those jobs go fast. You can also ask the larger chain stores that don't have jobs available if they know of any of their stores that are low on help.

## 6. Make Return Visits

It's not enough these days to just leave a résumé and hope the manager will get back to you. A lot of students have told me that they distributed 25 résumés in one day and no one phoned them. I ask them if they ever went back to the store again, and they said no. That, my friends, is the key. What you're seeking is a rapport with someone who's in the position to hire you. If they're not desperate for your help at the first visit, leave your résumé with them "in case something comes up," and check back at regular intervals.

When the manager says "We still don't have anything," smile and say "That's okay, just checking, keep me in mind," and other manager-friendly phrases. You're demonstrating persistence, politeness, and an easy-going nature, as well as embedding your existence into their memory. This pays off eventually.

Remember that although this feels horrible now, it'll pass when you have a job. Keep your head, your spirits, and your humour up. If you're totally nervous, take a trustworthy friend who'll wait outside the store in an inconspicuous place for you. Then if you get totally burned there's someone who you can laugh with about the snotty store help, and who'll pep-talk you (or shame you) into trying the next store. At the very least, end each day by treating yourself to a feet-up-on-the-sofa-watching-cheesy-videos kind of evening, or whatever you like to do that makes you feel good. You can handle this whole job-getting thing. Just make your own action.

Finally, don't ever give up the faith. A job can come along when you least expect it. Case in point:

# The Tale of the Couch Potato's Revenge

This story happened to a student named Vince when he was in high school. Summer had already begun and he'd made no effort to get a job. His mom walked into the den to find him comfortably ensconced on the sofa, clicker in hand, flipping through the channels with no remorse for his leisurely ways. This inspired Vince's mother to begin her umpteenth lecture about his, shall we say, unmotivated behaviour. "Do you actually think you're going to get a job sitting here on the sofa all day long? Nobody is just going to walk up to you and offer you a job, you have to get up off your rear end and go get one!" The lecture continued in this vein, which I won't describe because I'm sure most of us can imagine the content quite clearly.

The next day found our student still in the same position on the same sofa with the same remote glued to his palm. A neighbour walked into the house, saw Vince lying there, and asked "What are you doing right now?" Vince replied "Nothing," and the neighbour instantly said, "Hey, do you want to work for me this summer?" So by staying put and doing absolutely nothing whatsoever, Vince got himself a job at a drugstore for the entire summer. The best part was telling his mother.

You just never know.

CHAPTER 6

# Power Interviews

Good work, my friends, you've got an interview. Oh my god what are you going to do, you've got an interview. You're dead, man, you've got an interview. Wouldn't want to be in your shoes.

Interview time is looming and you're aware that you don't know what to say, and if you did you wouldn't know how to say it, and if you did you wouldn't know how to say it to be sure to get a job and if you did you wouldn't know how to dress anyway so what's the point.

There's no place you're more vulnerable in a job search than in an interview. You're in the room with the person who's going to make the decision about hiring you, and you can't get out until it's over. And you can't start again even if you don't like the way it's going.

There's also no other place in the job search where you have this much power. You have the ear of the person who's going to make the decision about hiring you, and for those uninterrupted (hopefully) five minutes to an hour, you have free licence to make yourself known and appreciated.

Interviews are scary stuff. I know. But I'm still here and together we're going to give you all the power you need to take your interview by storm. One of the first things to get is that, on some level, these people are trying to hire someone who they connect with, respond to, and think would understand how to fit into their work environment. This might be an odd coincidence, but being yourself is the fastest and easiest way to connect because then they'll sense that you're genuine and they'll believe what you have to say. And if they don't like you (say it with me) YOU WOULDN'T WANT TO WORK THERE ANYWAY.

## How Do I Go from Powerless to Powerful in My Interview?

Good question. I've told you that in an interview you're the most vulnerable you're going to be in this whole job search. I've also said that this is where you have the most power. Those of you who've been reading closely (Bill, stop staring out the window. Don't think I can't see you . . .) will have found a bit of a contradiction in those two statements. How can you be vulnerable and powerful at the same time?

The vulnerability comes from the fact that in order to get hired you have to show someone yourself and your abilities, and many of us find it hard to open up that way. We're all trained to guard ourselves; to protect our egos, our pride, and our self-esteem. And that kind of protection is important and useful, since when we feel safe we can interact in the world. Asking us to circumvent or minimize our defences is asking a lot. People don't like interviews because they've got to demonstrate themselves, and that's often an unprotected place. And yet the prospect of failure makes your defences feel necessary—you may not get the job.

The power comes from the preparation. If you've done the work through these past five chapters and continue in this one, you'll be able to walk through the vulnerable place with confidence because you won't be afraid of opening up and showing the employer who you are. This doesn't mean that you're fearless. Real courage isn't in being fearless, it's doing something in spite of your fear. It's realizing that if you're afraid, you're doing something that's really brave and that will actually get you somewhere. Without risk, there's no movement in life. You'll get power from risking because you'll see that there's no other way to get what you want . . . and you're not going to die if it doesn't happen.

All you have to do are three things:

- prepare yourself (using this chapter as a guide)
- show up at the interview
- speak what you've prepared.

That's all that has to happen. And you can handle it.

# What the Hell Am I Supposed to Say Anyway?

Let's get into the nitty-gritty basics of the interview. We're essentially going to work with the same concepts I've been yammering about since Chapter 1. Remember how we used those Crucial Questions to find specific examples to highlight in your résumé and cover letter? Well those stories, and others that were too long to explain there, are going to come in very handy for your interview.

I have an insider connection to the Human Resources department of a very large, very well-known bank, whose name I can't tell you because then I'd have to kill you. Hereafter I shall refer to it as "the Firm." You, my readers, are on a need-to-know basis only. My source, in deep undercover (dressed in typical office attire and a Mickey Mouse tie), smuggled out to me THE book, in a 50-cent orange duotang cover, that's used to interview potential job candidates. It outlines the questions that should be asked and the kinds of answers they're looking for. My Deep Throat (hereafter referred to by code name "Mickey Mouse") swears that the bank has trained all their hirers to interview according to this manual. And I'm going to divulge its secrets to you, because the information contained within its innocuous cover is power that will put you over the top. Follow my guidance and you will crush the competition.

## The "New" Interview

The manual talks about something called Behaviour-Focused Interviews. In secret job talk, this means that none of the questions can be answered by the word yes or no. I call them Give-A-Meritorious-Example interviews (so that we can hereafter refer to them as GAME interviews).

My job, as interview operative trainer, is to give you the best shot at competing in the interviewer's GAME. At the beginning of the manual the Firm lists what interviewers should be looking for:

1. *To seek candidates with the greatest future potential.*

   (Translation: Can you mop the floor well enough that I can eventually put you on the fryer?)

2. *There are core attributes, skills, values, and knowledge we need to look for in every new recruit.*

   (Translation: If the potential employee has never cleaned anything, can't follow directions, and hates being dirty, it's a safe bet that the mopping job is out.)

3. *Demonstrations of these core competencies are essential for successful performance.*

   (Translation: If the candidate can explain that at some point he or she was able to make something clean using a recognizable cleaning apparatus, we're on to something.)

Now what does the preceding mean to you, the bearer of this secret knowledge? One, the interviewer is looking for an employee who can do the job and who has the potential to do more. Two, in order to do the job, the potential employee (that's your code name, by the way) has to know and believe in basic stuff applying to the job that will allow you to do the job well. (For instance, core to the job of a lifeguard is the ability to guard the pool and save lives.) But secret ingredient number three is the key, because by now I'm sure you can handle numbers one and two. Number three means that the interviewer is *looking for proof* that you're truly able to fulfill numbers one and two. This is the GAME in a nutshell.

How do you "demonstrate core competencies essential for successful performance"? Easy. So easy I can tell you in one word: Examples. This is a translation of course from the top secret manual word for it, which is *behaviour*. Behaviour, and I'm paraphrasing here, describes what a person is doing, uses action verbs (check out the functional skills list at the back of this book), and can be heard, observed, experienced, and measured. In essence, the proof is in the pudding. Instead of telling the interviewer that you can do something, you demonstrate a time when your behaviour *showed* that you were doing it (remember Mrs. Corbett's advice from Chapter 3).

For example, pick out the things in the following description that demonstrate this person is competent:

> *I think I do a decent job. I'm pretty good with customers, especially difficult ones. Sometimes it's hard but I try to be polite. I try to offer other options; that's how I get around some difficulties. I have a lot of leeway at the store to make decisions. I think I do that well.*

Hard to determine exactly what makes this person good to hire, isn't it? Now try this version:

> *I'm very good with customers. For instance, Mr. Axe is a demanding customer, and whenever he calls I listen to his concerns and then take extra time to explain carefully what new books we're selling and to deal with his complaints. I answer each of his many questions patiently, and offer him options for the things he wants to buy. For instance, if we don't have the specific book he wants on medieval history, I offer other books on the same subject that are as good.*

Do you see the difference? In the second example, what specifically does this person do to deal with a difficult customer? She listens to him, she explains, she's patient, she answers his questions, she offers solutions to difficulties, and she uses her discretion to keep him happy with the store's service. I can hear, observe, and measure her performance in this example. To the Firm, this emphasizes her abilities much more dramatically than if she'd just said "I'm good with customers."

Meeting my undercover source one night, when we were yet again rendezvousing in another underground parking garage and he or she or whatever was smoking yet another cigarette and whispering corporate secrets to me, I asked what the theory behind all this example stuff was. After checking behind a few parked cars and scanning the elevators for bugs, Mickey Mouse told me the answer. *The best predictor of future performance is past performance in similar circumstances.* In other words, if you've done it once, chances are good that you'll do it again. That's why interviewers are looking to see if you've done it once already. Then I asked what that had to do with students who may not have done similar things, or have maybe even—horror of horrors—never done anything at all (job virgins, we call them). Mickey Mouse leaned real close—so close I could smell the double cappuccino on his/her breath—and growled, "Doesn't matter, they've all done something useful somewhere. They just gotta tell the interviewer what it was." Mickey Mouse then horked up something really disgusting, spat it on my shoe, and by the time I'd wiped it off with a Kleenex, he/she was gone.

"Aha!" I thought, ditching the Kleenex. "All I have to do is tell others how to tell others how they did something. Job virgins included." That became my mission.

## A Happy Note for Job Virgins

While I was riffling through the material Mickey Mouse left with me, I came upon a paragraph in the "Interviewer's Handy Guide" section of the book that you might be relieved to read. The paragraph said, and I quote,

> *When interviewing candidates who have no work-related experiences, encourage them to talk about non-work-related activities requiring similar behaviours. Remember that a person who has no directly acquired work-related experience might still be your best candidate for the job.*

Isn't that great? No lie, it's right there in black and white. Before we got started I just wanted you to know that there are people looking out for you.

# Questions,
# Questions, Questions

I know this is what you've all been waiting for—the cheat sheet of questions. I'm going to give you some different types of questions you may be asked and then show you ways of answering them. Then it's up to you to prepare the questions, because each of you, of course, will have different answers. Thankfully, all the work you've done up till now on your cover letter and résumé will help you out with that preparation. Still, nothing helps more than saying the answers to the questions out loud. As silly as this may sound (particularly to your family members, who'll be wondering who you're talking to in the shower), practising the answers polishes your thoughts and gets you comfortable with how you're going to explain your experience.

Here are some of the questions you might hear in an interview:

What's your name? How do you spell it?

How old are you?

Do you own a dog? What's its name?

What's your favourite colour? Orange?

Do you want this job?

When can you start?

Phew!

Those of us breathing a sigh of relief because we can handle these questions better keep reading. Although these kinds of questions can be asked, they usually don't comprise the major part of an interview. Basically, if people are going to pay you money, they're going to want to ask you some questions. Some tough questions. Whether you want to talk into a mirror or have a friend help you, practise, practise, practise.

Even Gandhi—one of the most influential humans in history, who led a whole country in peaceful civil disobedience, bringing the fighting in his country to a standstill and resulting in the British abandoning their rule—was afraid of public speaking. He spent hours in front of the mirror, practising his speeches. Can you imagine what would have happened if Gandhi hadn't practised, or if he hadn't spoken up because of his fear? History as we know it would not have been the same.

The main goal is to get really comfortable with what you're saying. That breeds a sense of confidence, and confidence makes for a good interview. Rather than sounding over-prepared, you'll end up knowing your own "material" well enough to bring it up in response to any variation of a question an interviewer could try on you. Thinking over your experience is even helpful on the trip to the interview. Anything is better than going in cold.

## "But I Need to Know the Questions Before I Can Practise the Answers"

Driving one day along a cliff road in Mickey Mouse's Aston Martin, trying to elude several black shiny limousines, I asked MM to reveal more information around "the plans"; specifically the kinds of questions that could come at you in an interview. Mickey finished riding the last limo off the cliff, and as it blew up in a loud fireball MM reached under the driver's seat and pulled out six Big Mac wrappers, as well as another section of the manual. This section, under the innocuous heading "Conducting the Interview," outlined the kinds of questions the interviewers ask. I inquired of MM if he/she thought there was one good way of answering interview questions. Looking into the distance Mickey pulled out a Marlboro, stuck it between his/her lips, and muttered, "The truth is out there," trying to hit the car's cigarette lighter in the process. Unfortunately he/she hit the ejector button instead, and I found myself airborne 50,000 feet above sea level. Luckily I was fastened in and the seat came with a parachute, so as I gently plummeted to the bottom of the mountain I read through the Question section.

## The Tough Questions

There are three tough questions that could be put to you on any given interview. You may get one of them, you may get them all, but in any case these are the questions to be best prepared for because they throw the greatest number of applicants. If there are any questions to be ready for, be ready for these.

### 1. The "Why Should We Hire You?" Question

Tell me about yourself.

"Tell me about yourself" is not an invitation to describe your age, height, and favourite flavour of ice cream. It's actually an invitation to tell the person in your own words why they should hire you. And let me warn you, I've had this question as an opener on more than one occasion. Sometimes it's used as a bit of a cop-out by the interviewer because they have no idea where to start and they're looking to you to provide them with relatedness, or something that both of you can talk about. The more aggressive interviewers will actually say "Why should we hire you?" as a kind of challenge. Have this sucker prepared and nothing can throw you.

You've got to consider this as your home-base question rather than as the enemy. Once you've worked out your answer you can use it as back-up in response to any form of the question. If you're ready for it, you can make your interview right here.

To answer this question, you have to be able to discuss a few skills or a few jobs that you've had, as they relate to the job you're interviewing for. So instead of telling them your shoe size and your favourite colour, you want to give them an overview of who you are in a job situation. Then you want to provide some proof. First off, however, you need some structure for answering the question. Once you've got the idea, and some practice, then you can improvise. Check out this question and response:

- restate the question
- give your idea/reasoning
- give an example illustrating your reason

Here's a question about how you'd handle a situation unique to the job. Check out the format of the answer:

*Do you believe discipline is important as a camp counsellor?*

*Yes I do believe discipline is important, and I'll tell you why. Camp is supposed to be a fun place, but it can't be fun if someone gets hurt. Discipline, in proportion to the misbehaviour, is appropriate to keep kids from getting hurt. For instance, I babysat two six-year-old twins. I let them run around in the backyard playing super heroes because that's their favourite game. I'll even play it with them. But at one point the twins were jumping off the swing set, trying to imitate flying. I asked them to stop, and when they didn't I brought them into the house and explained that as good as it felt, they could hurt themselves and that would make me sad. They could play inside until they were ready to agree that if they played outside they wouldn't jump off the swing. Within ten minutes they agreed to my request, and then played happily outside. To make them feel better I gave them airplane rides. So you see, discipline saved them from being seriously hurt, but it didn't take the fun out of the afternoon.*

Notice how much richer the answer gets when our potential employee gets into the example. That's where the actual meat of the answer is. As an interviewer, I can determine from the example exactly how this person is going to deal with my campers. If I want a counsellor who recognizes the need for safety and for setting limits without ruining the day's fun, I have a pretty good potential counsellor on my hands. And further, I believe this person because I know the specifics. It's harder to make up these kinds of details.

There's also the type of question that asks you to demonstrate a skill. The answer again follows the same format:

*Do you consider yourself organized?*

*Yes, I consider myself exceptionally organized, and I say this because that's the way I have to be for my own sanity. I find that there's usually a more efficient way to do most tasks, and that a little bit of organization off the top will save you time later. Also, if something is organized clearly, everybody knows how to access information more quickly and everyone benefits. When I worked as an office filer, it was my suggestion to colour code the files into active, non-active, and urgent. That saved the managers a lot of time trying to decide how to prioritize the files on their desks without going through every one. I do this everywhere. Even at my volunteer job at the radio station, I stayed late to re-label all the tapes so that people could read them more clearly. I'm always finding ways of making my work area more organized.*

If you're a job virgin, or if you're applying for a job for which you have absolutely no previous experience, the third part of the process (the giving-an-example part) can literally save your interview.

*Tell me about a time you went out of your way for a customer.*

*Although I don't have any direct retail experience, I believe it's important to give 100 percent to anything you do. For example, there are a few elderly people in my neighbourhood who can't shovel their walkways. I know that they could slip and fall if the walks didn't get shovelled, so several times after the heavy snows I went and did it for them. I didn't get paid for it, but one lady had me in for hot chocolate. I think that relates to what you're asking though, because I went out of my way to help people who couldn't do it themselves. I'm good at anticipating what people need.*

Again, see how the lack of retail experience is minimized by pointing out the parallels with other jobs or volunteer work you've done. You can't control the questions you'll be asked, but you *can* control the information you give back as a response. That, my friends, is the name of the GAME.

So tell me about yourself. Are you organized, precise, and focused? Are you a people person who works well in a team? Do you like physical work for long hours? Look back to the end of Chapter One. What were your skills? What did you like to do? That's who you are and what I want to know when I ask, "Tell me about yourself."

## 2. The "Why Us?" Question

This question is usually phrased "Why do you want to work here?" It's a demonstration that you care where you get the job, and that you understand what the job will entail. This is the kind of question that will get you eliminated from the word go if they don't like your answer. Sometimes the "screener" is a pre-interview which, like these other techniques, is designed to get rid of undesirables. What's undesirable? Answering the question "Why do you want to work at the Gap?" with a sentence anything like "Well, I was just walking by the store and I saw the sign outside and I decided to come in 'cause I needed a job . . . and what exactly do you sell again?"

Before you go in, think about the advantages of the particular store, camp, restaurant, or company. Do you wear their clothes, like their windows, or know about their policies with animal testing? Is it a company that you know something about, is it a business that matches one of your hobbies? This is a question that may need research, or that may be as simple as your own opinion. Check out these two examples. Remember that these don't necessarily have to be one-sided speeches. In fact, there's plenty of room for an interviewer to jump in and agree, to clarify, and to back up these points:

*This is my favourite clothing company because I love the fact that you change the selection every two weeks. I realize that this must be a lot of work, considering most stores only change their stock every season, but that makes your store worth visiting at least once or twice a month. For instance, in my own experience, I came here and bought my basic fall clothes: two pairs of the cigarette pants that are big this season, and two thin sweaters that are interchangeable. I thought I was done! But two weeks later you had a cardigan in the window that went with everything I'd just bought, and when I walked in the store I saw at least five major items that hadn't been there before. I'd like to work for a store that has that much selection. It would be interesting for me because I wouldn't get tired of selling the same old thing, and it would also be another reason to encourage the customers to come back soon and mean it.*

Throughout this answer you get several things loud and clear: this person knows her clothes, she knows her seasons, and she knows what this store has to offer. And she's talking about something she's very comfortable with. At the end, she pulls her opinion together to mean something about why she'd want to work in the store. And her answers make her both human and a potentially great salesperson.

What happens if you don't know that much about the place that's hiring? Use your powers of observation:

*I've loved horses for ten years and I've heard that your stables have a great reputation for being good to the horses. When I walked through the stables before the interview, I was pleased to see that the stalls had plenty of room and that everything was so clean. I feel strongly that horses should be groomed every day and that stalls should be more than mucked out, they should be washed out every day too. It makes the horses happier and the stables more appealing. I also really like all the space you've left in the grooming areas. I've tried to groom horses in the narrow space in front of the stalls, and you can never get the job done properly because everyone's always trying to press by you and the horses can get nervous and fidgety. It makes me feel good about the possibility of working here, because you put the horses' comfort first, like I do.*

The speaker here uses what she's seen in the stables maybe five, ten minutes before the interview to back up the reputation she's only heard about. (A note of warning: saying "I've heard you've got a great reputation/store/company" is a dead-ender if you have nothing to back it up with. The interviewer's natural follow-through is "Oh really? What have you heard?" and if you haven't really heard anything, or even anything specific, you, my friend, are a sitting duck.) This version takes more spontaneity, and I'm going to bet this person was prepared when she arrived at the stables, because instead of focusing on what she was going to say

she was looking around her to see if *she* liked the potential job. The interview isn't all one-sided, you know. You're making a decision too.

So for these kinds of answers, you want to think about what was the thing that triggered you into deciding you wanted to work at this place. Can you think of the exact moment? Then set up the scene for the interviewer—tell the story. "When I'm on the Net I'd always find that my favourite site was yours, and one day it hit me that . . . blah blah blah." Make it the truth and make it specific.

## Girls in Short Skirts Who Kiss Bouncers Tend to Get into Nightclubs Faster

While we're on the subject of the "Why Us?", mass hiring will often have what's called a "screener." The manual describes the pre-screen as "narrowing for the best fit." This means that the interviewers are trying to condense the field to people who already sound as though they could be a match for the job. In some cases, the pre-screen is a written application, like the one I did for my video store, in which you're writing down the GAME instead of speaking it to someone. Sometimes the pre-screen is as simple as looking at your available hours and then deciding to see you because your schedule matches theirs.

There are other tricky tools that employers use in order to weed out undesirables. For instance, some big chains who mass-hire will put a person on the door to hand out applications. Little do you know it, but he or she is actually a planted employer representative who's judging how you interact with the regular folk (read: other people) who are not your (potential) boss. Remember how I said in the last chapter to be nice to receptionists and personal assistants? Let me qualify that: be nice to everybody, including the dog. Conduct yourself as if the interview starts the moment you walk into the building, not the moment you actually meet the interviewer.

## 3. The "What Are Your Strengths/One of Your Weaknesses?" Questions

I think you can handle the "What are your strengths?" question. Think back to all the skill stuff we've been talking about. Prepare that question in a set of three skills, both functional and personality. For instance, you could choose organized, efficient, and fun; or creative, motivated, and communicative. Check the back of the book for suggestions. And think about what the job requires as you pick your positive qualities. Then get a story or a specific demonstration of that behaviour to back up each point, as in the previous examples.

The question that usually stumps people is "What is one of your weaknesses?" And chocolate is not an answer. Neither is "My weakness is that I tend to work too hard." Or worse, "I have no weaknesses." So all you wise guys out there better think about this one.

Here's the format. All weaknesses are a strength, all strengths are a weakness. So when you answer the question, you want to present your weakness, show how it can be useful, and discuss how you handle it when it comes up for you. For instance:

> *A weakness I have is impatience. I get irritated when I feel that things aren't running efficiently and people are wasting time. My impatience can actually be a good thing because I tend to get people on track again, but I often have trouble accepting the process of getting a job done. One of the ways I handle my impatience is to voice it to others in a constructive way. For instance, I was at a School Council meeting and we'd spent nearly an hour on the subject of whether or not to invest in new school bathing suits. I was getting really irritated and not paying attention, when*

*I caught myself and decided to speak up. I just raised my hand and said, "I feel like we've been through these arguments thoroughly and that we can all consider them fully. Does anyone have any objection to having a final vote on this subject at the next meeting?" It got us out of the impasse, and by the next meeting the Head of the Council had a bit more information that helped us to make the decision. I've found that my impatience lets me know that something different has to happen.*

Wow. This guy shows us his weakness (actually two: he gets impatient and then he gets irritated—even worse!) and then makes it seem like the best thing that ever happened to him. Why? He uses his weakness as an access point for action. He gets power out of being an impatient and irritated person. But note his example carefully. He doesn't *act* impatient and irritated, that's just how he feels. He uses those feelings to note when he needs to act positively. The difference is subtle but very important. You don't have to be having a temper tantrum to be angry, or hide in a corner to be scared. You can just have that weakness within yourself, that you may indulge in from time to time, but when you become aware of your feelings you can use them to change something (i.e. voicing what's upsetting you, or taking on the challenge that's scaring you).

You really have to think about this question because it's going to feel hard at first to make your weakness sound good. Keep in mind the power of vulnerability when it's manifested at opportune moments. A person who can admit weaknesses is a genuine, human person who's comfortable to be around because they don't pretend to be perfect. This question is a good place to show a little of that humanness. My only caution is not to swing too far the other way and start reciting a litany of horrible character and work traits. Don't go overboard with this "I'm human" thing. You need to give this conversation a lot of context, because the interviewer doesn't know you well enough to know your innermost secrets. The context (the example) will let them know how you use your weakness to advantage.

## Next Up: The Behaviour-Oriented Questions

The manual outlined these questions as the ones that elicit a specific example in their answer. In fact these questions are *designed* to get a specific example out of you. If an interviewer asks you this kind of question, they've been properly trained in the art of interviewing, and they expect the kind of answers I've been showing you how to formulate. Some of these questions are biased toward customer service, but you can substitute job-specific details for the same questions. Test these examples out on yourself:

Describe a time when you provided a service to another person.

Describe a time when you promoted a product or service by explaining its potential benefits relative to a person's need.

Describe a time when you worked as part of a team to accomplish common goals.

Describe a mistake from which you learned a valuable lesson.

Describe a time that you failed at something and what you learned.

Describe a time you had to follow instructions or directions.

Tell me about a time when you were mad at your boss. What did you do?

Notice that these aren't even questions in the traditional question mark sense. The person who asks these may even probe you further to get to the heart of how you did the job.

## Hypothetical and Other Job-Specific Questions

These are the ones that deal specifically with the job or industry you're applying for. Students have told me about questions in interviews that are framed as hypothetical situations, such as "You have a group of ten seven-year-old kids, and one kid is misbehaving badly and disturbing the rest of the group. What do you do?" What was throwing these students was that they could feel that the interviewer wanted a specific answer, and they weren't sure what it was.

In any interview you're going to get the feeling that the interviewer is looking for a particular answer, and you're (quite humanly) going to want to figure out what it is. The problem is that you're not a mind reader, you're a student who wants a job. So I suggest that—big surprise—you answer the question as honestly as you can, knowing that if they don't hire you because they'd rather have someone who disciplines differently, you probably wouldn't want to work there.

A good tip however is to watch for the ethical dilemma type questions, such as "You're told by a camper that she's been touched sexually by another camper. What do you do?" If you aren't sure what's right or wrong and it feels overwhelming, they're probably looking to see if you'd know to ask your boss, camp director, or manager for advice if you were in over your head. So if you feel completely torn on a question like that, your fallback can always be "I'd go ask my manager for his or her help."

I recommend that you give some thought before the interview to any job-specific questions of this nature you might get. Certainly you should be up on what's happening in that field. My own publisher was amazed at the summer student applicants she stumped with the question "What have you been reading recently?" If you're applying to a publisher, read some books. If you're applying to a video store, know some new releases. You get the idea.

## More Questions

Here's a list of some of the more straightfoward questions that you might get in an interview. Use the principles I've explained to help you answer them.

Why do you feel you'd like this job?

How did you find out about this job?

What do you know about this company?

Why do you feel that you'd be a good candidate for this job?

Do you have any experience related to this job?

Do you know of any negative aspects of this job?

What subjects do you like the most? Why?

What subjects do you do best in?

What interests or hobbies do you have?

What jobs have you held?

What sorts of volunteer work have you done?

Who do you feel has influenced you the most in your life?

How do you feel you've been treated by previous bosses?

What sorts of books do you read?

How much career planning have you done?

How do you get along with your peers? Adults? Younger children?

What qualities do you value most in a job?

What sort of boss do you prefer?

Do you like to work alone or as part of a team?

What do you feel is your most outstanding accomplishment?

What do you generally do during the summer?

Have you taken any courses or programs apart from your daily school program?

Do you feel you have leadership skills?

Have you had any leadership roles in the past?

Have you earned any money? How?

What do you want out of life?

Why did you choose the school you're attending?

How is being a student going to help you in this job?

What extracurricular activities do you do?

What special skills do you have for this job?

Do you like to work with things/data/people?

Are you aggressive/assertive?

Are you ambitious?

Why do you want this job?

How soon can you start working?

Would you work overtime?

How would this company benefit from hiring you?

Do you have any questions?

What are your goals this summer?

## No Further Questions . . . Please!

Good news. That's about it for the questions. Now mind you, interviewers are always coming up with the weirdest stuff, and you're just going to have to do your best with what they throw at you. The thing is that if you're really prepared, you can begin to work any question back to your main points. I always coach people to have a home-base answer about who they are. You'll find that you can lead pretty much any question back "home."

*What books have you been reading lately?*

*I'm glad you said books, because I tend to read more than one at a time. I find I like to read a book based on my mood. So for instance, right now I'm reading a business book called* Strategy of the Dolphin, *which is amazing for how to cooperate in the workplace. I'm also reading the new Sue Grafton mystery, and every night I read a few more sections from Dante's* Divine Comedy. *It's slow going, but it's worth the work. I find that I need a lot of stimulation to keep me interested, and I enjoy viewing things from different perspectives. That's why I'd be so excited to work in your company—there's always so much going on and so many new things happening, and I feel capable of keeping track of it all.*

*I've just been reading one book recently,* Moby Dick. *I decided to read it because it demands a lot of focus and attention from the reader to get the whole story. When Melville starts in on a twenty-page description of whales, I stick to reading all of it in detail, even though it's sometimes difficult to concentrate. That's how I know that I can work at this office, because if I can focus on* Moby Dick, *I can handle anything you throw me!*

Same question, different home base. Once you know your stuff, these interviews are going to be all yours.

## Interview Basics

This stuff is so basic they don't even put it in the manual. I won't waste your time by going into these points in detail, since I know you're intelligent enough to figure out the theory behind them. Your brilliant interview will be greatly benefited if you:

- Arrive on time (which is five to ten minutes early).
- Attend to personal hygiene.
- Arrive without five friends to accompany you.
- Bring your résumé, references, and anything else applicable.
- Don't chew gum.
- Look calm, cool, and collected.

Phew! I betcha thought that'd take longer.

### Absolute No Nos

- Answering your cell phone while in the interview.
- When asked about loyalty, showing your tattoo.
- Coming back later and asking if you can re-do the interview.

- Leaving the room to meditate.
- Making the interviewer switch chairs with you.
- When asked to take your time, writing down all your answers.

You think I'm crazy? These things actually happened. The motto here is: Think like a sane person.

## Best-Day Rule of Dress

This piece of advice for how to dress for an interview was the best I ever received. Everyone will give you the "suit and tie, nice skirt and jacket" advice, but this doesn't take into account all the different kinds of jobs out there. You'd be laughed out of the office if you showed up to a tree-planting interview in a power suit. They'd think you'd wandered into the wrong interview by mistake. So here's the advice:

*Dress for the best day on the job.*

Pretty good, huh? In this way, you're sure of matching the clothes to the specific job. In all cases, keep your clothing on the simple side. You don't need a lot of flashy colour, or jewellery, or head-turning tight-fitting apparel. You want to be doing the talking, not your clothes.

## The International Language

As you may know from biology or sociology, body language is often read more clearly by others than the actual words you say. For instance, your hand grabbing your throat is the international sign for choking. Your hand grabbing someone else's throat, however, is the international sign for "I'm going to kill my roommate because she keeps playing that Tori Amos CD over and over again." Maybe the second one isn't translated exactly that way worldwide, but you get the general gist.

As well as all those words, examples, and stories floating around in your head, make room for checking that your body language is reflecting a confident, capable, and charming you, as opposed to a scared, snivelly, and slobbering you.

How do you act with confidence when you're nervous? Well, if you can't feel confident, act "as if" you are. For a refresher, confident people: walk and sit upright, have a firm but warm handshake, say "hello" and "pleasure to meet you," look people in the eye when talking to them, and say a clear "thank you" and "goodbye" on exiting.

Try a few little meditation-type techniques (without actually contorting yourself on the waiting room chair and starting to chant) to keep your body relaxed, which says confidence. Right before your name is called, clear your mind of all interview confusion, and take three deep breaths. Let the air sink in below the diaphragm and exhale completely (but quietly, you don't want to scare the receptionist). When you're sitting in the interview chair, relax your shoulders from your ears, and begin answering questions.

Above all, don't forget to smile. Obviously you don't want to be grinning like a schmuck throughout the whole interview, but in order to create a rapport with the interviewer, and signal your open, positive attitude, a smile helps to make the conversation seem more like a dialogue and like you want to be there.

## Where the Power Is (You!)

So that's how to handle your interview. Do you feel better? If you said no, go start practising. If you said yes, great, go practise some more.

## And So I Take My Leave . . .

You've done it! Congratulations. Now get working. And remember, if you feel like goofing off a little, you've earned it, but you may need references for next year, so don't go too crazy.

As for Mickey Mouse, now that his/her job as spy is done, I know he/she's out there crossing the border with fake identification, and starting a goat farm somewhere in South America, far from the long arm of The Secret Clan Of Interviewers. The last words he/she croaked to me were "Do up your zipper, you're flying low," and for that, Mickey Mouse, wherever you are, I'm grateful.

And now this chapter draws to a close. I've been your guide through the perils of job hunting. It's up to you now. Still, whether or not you get a job, you're okay just as you are right now. Steve and I will be thinking of you.

PART 2

# JOBS YOU'LL LOVE, JOBS YOU'LL HATE, AND JOBS YOU'VE NEVER THOUGHT OF

Me and my extraordinary researcher Nicole (who's had her phone glued to her hand for the last six months) have come up with over fifty jobs that you could get this summer, along with some of the crucial information that you'll need in order to a) decide if the job's for you, and b) how to apply for it. Nicole and I spoke to a lot of students, some of whose comments you can read here. We've created this job smorgasbord so that you can sample variations on all different kinds of work. Pretty nice of us, huh?

But in no way is this the final say on any of these jobs, or on student jobs in general. (I'm sure there are a ton more, and I'm also sure that I'll go crazy if I think of another one.) So you've still got to find the proper phone numbers and contact names, or do your own legwork to discover other options and ideas. This is your job search; I'm just here to make it more colourful.

The jobs are broken down into different sections, and each job has a code at the top. As you're scanning the codes, remember that these are only estimates, since I can't summarize when all the provincial parks will be hiring or how much every gas station pays. (It's just like how I can't do the interview for you—it sucks, but there you are.)

Nicole and I are going to take a nap while you read on. Happy job shopping!

Indoor or outdoor work (or both)

Under minimum wage or no money at all

Around minimum wage

Above minimum wage by a dollar or more, to about $10 an hour

Above $10 an hour

JAN The month you should definitely start applying for summer work

You can apply any time for this job, since it can be part-time work year-round

# WORKING WITH ANIMALS

*"You can expect most classes of bodily fluid to come in contact with you on this job."*

***—Derek (vet assistant)***

*"You don't play with puppies all day. It's work."*

***—Charlene (pet groomer)***

*"What I like is the smell of the horse s—t; it has an aroma in the morning that is indescribable."*

***—Clint (stable hand)***

## Animal Care Attendant, Vet Assistant, and Pet Groomer's Assistant

**Age:** From 15 to 18, depending on the situation
**Pay:** Depending on the type of work, the money can range from non-existent to excellent
**Dress Code:** Something that you don't mind having covered in hair, saliva, and other animal residue
**Job Prospects:** Fair to Good
**What to Expect:** There are many variations on jobs that can put you in close contact with animals and give you the responsibility for their well-being. The basic tenets of the job are the same: you'll be cleaning and disinfecting their living environments, preparing food, bathing, trimming, or clipping animals, and generally observing their behaviour to find out if they're well and properly cared for. These duties exist in such jobs as animal shelter attendants, kennel attendants, stable workers (see below), aquarists (that's fish), pet shop attendants, and laboratory animal technicians.

If you're the type of person who thinks a dog is very nice to pat on the head, and then you wish it would go away and play somewhere, this kind of job is not for you. Particularly in the case of the pet shop worker and lab technician, you can expect to get attached to animals that you may never see again. You're going to have to deal with a family you hate picking the puppy you love, or you're going to have to endure the rabbit you love being poked with a needle twice a day, and you'll be holding her.

Vet assistant is a combination of office clerking and animal handling. Unless you're specifically hired for behind-the-scenes animal work, most vet assistants also help to file, book appointments, do paperwork, and anything else that vets don't like doing. For this portion of the job, any general office skills will do.

As a pet groomer's assistant you'll also most likely be doing office and retail work, such as booking appointments, making change, and greeting customers. You'll be learning how to make Fluffy look good, without being scratched or bitten too much. You may get regular animals that need a touch-up on their poofy dog-do, or you may get really tough customers that haven't had a bath since their last sixteen swims in the local lake.

**What's Expected of You:** Consistency with the animals, and decent, humane treatment (if not, you can report the store or lab immediately).

**Required Knowledge Skills:** Some knowledge of animals will be helpful, if not downright necessary. The employers want to know that you're going to be an asset with their creatures, not an addition to chaos. Number one however, is that you must have respect for the animals.

**Where to Get Started:** Depending on which route you want to take, you're looking at cold calls and personal visits to places that involve animals—pet shops, kennels, labs, even zoos. If you think you need more experience to do that, try volunteering at a local animal shelter to get a feel for caring for a large number of animals. Another possibility is to care for someone's pets while they're away.

Connections here would be great, but you could also check employment centres and newspapers for any animal-related jobs. For more information on this general area of work, and some possible places to approach in your area, you could contact the places below.

Canadian Council on Animal Care
350 Albert Street, Suite 315, Ottawa, ON K1R 1B1 (613) 238-4031

Canadian Kennel Club
89 Skyway Avenue, Suite 100, Etobicoke, ON M9W 6R4 (416) 675-5511

The Canadian Veterinary Medical Association
339 Booth Street, Ottawa, ON K1R 7K1 (613) 236-1162

# Stable Hand

**Age:** Usually 16
**Pay:** Very little to $300 a week (rarely hourly pay)
**Dress Code:** Mucking-out clothing (things you don't mind getting really dirty)
**Job Prospects:** Fair
**What to Expect:** If you've considered this job at all, you've considered it an honour and a privilege to be so close to the creatures you love. But if you're at all like me and you've read every fiction and non-fiction horse book you could find since the age of nine, you may want to investigate whether your love of horses is purely literary or really really really what you want to do.

Part of your job may be to ride a horse or two and give them a decent workout (or maybe even continue their training). This is probably the reason you can stand mucking out all those stables—for that moment when you can finally sit on a horse.
**What's Expected of You:** A willingness to do anything for a horse.
**Required Knowledge Skills:** How to shovel. How to walk around a horse without being kicked. How to talk horses with other horsey people. Perhaps the most insightful tip is encapsulated in the stable hand phrase "Drunken grooms and rainy days make the best horsemen." The message is not that you should be drinking shots of tequila in the barn, but rather that the more relaxed you are around horses, the better a groom you'll be.
**Where to Get Started:** There's a huge range of horses and horse-related activities for you to choose from: working with show horses at fancy stables, thoroughbreds at a racetrack, a breeding farm with mares and their colts, a teaching stable where tired hacks haul kids around, a jumping school, or working with those ever-excitable polo ponies.

To do this job you need experience around horses, which means that you've either grown up around them, or taken lots of lessons, or you've volunteered. Volunteering is a great way to get started. Go to farms, stables, or racetracks and offer your assistance. If the main office doesn't take you on, there may be a horse owner willing to sponsor your being there if you clean their stables and exercise their horse for them. Just be willing to learn, and when you've got it down pat, ask to be paid. (If you're still volunteering and you're essentially taking care of the stables, you're being used.) This experience will help you get paid work.

## Dog Walker

**Age:** 13
**Pay:** Anywhere from $3 a dog to $40 a week
**Dress Code:** Anything you like, the dog doesn't care
**Job Prospects:** Excellent if you're willing to advertise
**What to Expect:** Walking. Poop scooping, feeding, newspaper changing, and love and tenderness may also be involved, especially if the owners are away and Lassie's feeling lonely.
**What's Expected of You:** You'll probably be entrusted with the key to the owner's house as well as their dog, which could represent anything from their protector to their only child. You might be the only human that dog sees all day, so show it some love and compassion.
**Where to Get Started:** Either knock on dog owners' doors, or meet up with them as they're walking their animals and offer your services. Use current babysitting rates as a guide to how you should be paid (either per hour, per dog, or per walk; whatever's applicable to your situation).

# WORKING WITH ARTSIES

*"Essentially it comes down to talent. But even a great actor can lose a job because they don't display the right amount of professionalism."*
***—Thea (acting and modelling)***

*"You have to be totally insane to do what I do."*
***—DJ Rick***

*"It almost killed me but I enjoyed it. Expect to work way more than you're paid."*
***—Dan (theatre production)***

# Film Production

**Age:** 18
**Pay:** For PA (production assistant), typically $120–140 a day
**Dress Code:** Casual working cool
**Job Prospects:** Good luck
**What to Expect:** Leave your film texts at home 'cause nobody's listening to you, certainly not at this rung of the ladder. You're entering the jungle of the movie set, a circus full of tension, drama, gossip, politics, and often utter boredom. Have you ever been on a movie set? Directors take and re-take and re-take the same scene sometimes to the godawful number of 67 takes. Between takes there's a lot of down time as the next scene is set up, lit, rehearsed, and then thrown out for the day because the actor has a problem with a line of dialogue.

On the other hand, you're also part of what can be a tight little crew, as the film set begins to function as a family home and the participants bond together through trials and successes. The fact that you're doing nothing more interesting than turning traffic away from the street shoot, or holding the second assistant director's clipboard for her as she tears her hair out, becomes fun and exciting in the glamour world of movie making.

Although 120 bucks a day may seem like a lot, the shoots often require you to be present for eighteen hours straight. Don't kid yourself, when a movie is shooting there are few days off and no social life to speak of (hence the set replacing that function). On the other hand, the wrap party can be wildly outrageous and you get to see your name in the credits of *Bloodthirst 5: The Nightmare Never Ends.*
**What's Expected of You:** Your blood, sweat, loyalty, and cheery demeanour, despite the fact that you'll be treated like a cross between a workhorse and a trained seal. Remember that if you have any designs to be in film (and why else would you be doing what's essentially a slave job?), keep your cool and keep your happy face. Think of it this way: if you have to spend most of your life on a closed set for eighty hours a week, wouldn't you rather spend it with people you get along with? Do the grunt work without losing your smile or your backbone, and the chances of getting re-hired (and for a better job) are pretty good.

**Required Knowledge Skills:** How to make coffee. How to run with hot coffee. How to order a proper latte. How to chew out someone lower than you for not properly ordering a latte.

**Where to Get Started:** You're most likely to get a job if you're in a city where movies actually get made. In other words, for the most part this kind of job is very Toronto-Vancouver-Montreal-centric. Still, you never know when that big production is going to roll into your town because it's got just that look the director's been searching for since she read the screenplay.

This field is highly connections-oriented, so here's hoping you have a neighbour/gardener/friend/relative/parent in the business. Use the research section in Chapter 4 to help you discover the production houses nearest you. The most obvious place to find them is through the Yellow Pages under Motion Picture Producers & Studios. Blanketing offices with your résumé probably won't be too much help. You've got to be ultra-persistent. Make friends in offices by phoning every week and leaving friendly, I-want-to-be-your-slave messages. Someone in "the biz" recommended to me that you get a business card and a pager number, go to where a film is shooting, and hand it out. You never know when an overwrought techie might need a hand. Another tactic is to offer your services free for a summer, become indispensable, and then they'll want you back.

Film festivals beget film people and thus connections are born. If you're a little shy about meeting people in a movie lineup, try working for one of the festivals. Then you'll have a reason to chat to the big names.

Toronto International Film Festival
2 Carleton St., Toronto, ON M5B 1J3
(416) 967-7371

Greater Vancouver International Film Festival Society
#410-1008 Homer St., Vancouver, BC V6B 2X1
(604) 685-0260

le Festival international du cinéma et des nouveaux média de Montréal
3668, boul St. Laurent, Montreal, PQ H2X 2V4
(514) 843-4725

# Theatre Production

**Age:** 17
**Pay:** Summer stock—working for very little, room and board plus gratuity; Actors—possible deficit
**Dress Code:** For administrative jobs, low-key office wear; for actual production, jeans and T-shirts
**Job Prospects:** Good
**What to Expect:** You can expect to work like a dog. Theatre is a grimy, grungy, wipe-the-sweat-off-your-brow kinda world. Whether you're in the office trying to pull a whole production season together financially, out in "the shop" building a set that'll be torn down in two weeks, in the theatre learning the lighting board for a whole new show, writing down the director's every blocking whim, or even just ushering a thousand people to their seats, you'll be working hard.

Actors in particular should heed this warning, because in summer stock they get passed around from woodcutting to stamp licking in between rehearsals for *Rockin' Little Red Riding Hood*. Actors often don't get paid because it's their privilege to earn Equity points. Be sure to get details and ask how others have survived.

The key to the whole notion of working in theatre (particularly the smaller summer stock theatres) is that they're always understaffed. Therefore, you can expect to get more responsibility thrown your way than if you were doing any other kind of summer job. Whether you're in administration or acting it's likely that, unless you're working for the Stratford Festival, you'll be doing more than your job description.

On the production side of things, expect to work 14 to 16-hour days whatever your job description. The credo of summer stock production crews is "build to burn." As soon as you set up one set, you've got less than a week to set up the next.
**What's Expected of You:** That you either know what you're doing or that you're ready to learn it fast.
**Where to Get Started:** Basically, you need to contact theatres in your area, or across Canada, to see if they'll take you for the summer. These places will need people, especially if they're not big festivals like the Shaw, which have bigger budgets and are more difficult to get into.

At this level in your acting career most places like head shots, but an agent isn't necessary. Get yourself some good audition monologues and only do Shakespeare if they require it.

Theatre associations have publications that list the phone numbers of different theatres and the names of the artistic directors. Some of these associations may even have a job board, where you can look up theatres advertising for the summer. Some universities have job fairs, where hiring theatres send representatives to entice you to work there.

Theatre Alberta
Percy Page Centre, 3rd Fl.
11759 Grant Rd., Edmonton, AB T5M 3K6
(403) 422-8162

British Columbia Drama Association
Theatre BC
307-1005 Broad St., Victoria, BC V8W 2A1
(604) 381-2443

CCYDA—Drama Canada
Canadian Child & Youth Drama Association
8999 McAllister Rd., P.O. Box 969, Fort Langley, BC V0X 1J0

Canadian Actor's Equity Association (CLC)
Association canadienne des artistes de la scène (CTC)
260 Richmond St. East, 2nd Fl., Toronto, ON M5A 1P4
(416) 867-9165

National Multicultural Theatre Association (NMTA)
Nova Scotia Drama League
1809 Barrington St., Ste. 901, Halifax, NS B3T 3K8
(902) 425-3876

Popular Theatre Alliance of Manitoba (PTAM)
393 Portage Ave., Unit Y300, Winnipeg, MB R3B 3H6
(204) 957-5425

Prairie Theatre Exchange (PTE)
393 Portage Ave., Unit Y300, Winnipeg, MB R3B 3H6
(204) 942-7291

Professional Association of Canadian Theatre/Association professionnelle des theatres canadiens (PACT)
415 Yonge St., Ste. 1500, Toronto, ON M5B 2E7
(416) 595-6455, Toll-Free 1-800-263-7228

Saskatchewan Drama Association
203-2135 Albert St., Regina, SK S4P 2V1
(306) 525-0151

Theatre Network Society
10708-124 St., Edmonton, AB T5M 0H1
(403) 453-2440

Theatre New Brunswick (TNB)
The Playhouse, P.O. Box 566, Fredericton, NB E3B 5A6
(506) 458-8345

Theatre Ontario
415 Yonge St., Ste. 1500, Toronto, ON M5B 2E7
(416) 964-6771

Theatre Prince Edward Island
550 University Ave., Charlottetown, PE C1A 4P3
(902) 566-0321

Theatre associes inc. (TAI)
260, boul. de Maisonneuve ouest, Montréal, PQ H2X 1Y9
(514) 842-6361

Two big festivals to consider are:

Stratford Shakespearean Festival Foundation of Canada
55 Queen St., P.O. Box 520, Stratford, ON N5A 6V2
Toll-Free 1-800-567-1600

Shaw Festival Theatre Foundation
P.O. Box 774, Niagara on the Lake, ON L0S 1J0
(905) 468-2153

# Acting (Film and Television)

**Age:** Any age
**Pay:** Very good (principle actors/actresses get paid in the $350-400 range per 5 to 6 hours, depending on experience and the union rates), as long as you get work
**Dress Code:** Whatever the part demands
**Job Prospects:** Excellent if you're Brad Pitt, otherwise Good Luck

**What to Expect:** You could wind up in an incredibly supportive atmosphere where they listen to your suggestions and encourage you to plumb the depths of your actor's soul to fit the part, or you could arrive for work on a bitter, nasty, and unsupportive set, where the director huddles in his trailer and only comes out to yell action, and the crew are quitting in crowds of ten.

It's an exciting, thrilling life that some people would give their grandmother to participate in, but the people who make it are the ones most committed to living the uncertain lifestyle.

**What's Expected of You:** Often directors like people who've experienced being on a set and in front of a camera, so you may get caught for a while in the "I need to get hired to get experience" dilemma that traps so many people.

Be prepared to work long, long hours. In shooting a beer commercial an old friend of mine went through 82 takes of the same line, and he had to laugh in the same spot with conviction every single time. Meryl Streep stood on a mountain top in a scene from *Out of Africa* and cried for a series of twenty takes. It's a draining job, but if the end product is good, it'll be worth the pain.

**Required Knowledge Skills:** Acting for a camera is different from acting for theatre. Go see a play and then rent some movies to see the differences. The camera takes you in closer, so less is more. Check out Acting for Film classes.

**Where to Get Started:** The number one thing that you need is an agent. A reputable agent shouldn't require you to pay money, take classes, or have a test shoot. Their fee shouldn't be paid up front; it should be deducted as you earn money. Their rate is typically around 15 percent. You'll need references from any parts you've played previously. Ask a theatre or drama school for references, or call different agencies and ask them what they can offer you. Another idea is to ask local actors for their advice.

A.C.T.R.A.—Alliance of Canadian Cinema Television & Radio Artists
(union for performing artists)
* will have lists of agents
2239 Yonge Street, Toronto, ON M4S 2B5
(416) 489-1311

Edmonton (403) 433-4090
Calgary (403) 228-3123
Regina (306) 757-0885
Winnipeg (204) 943-1307
Ottawa (613) 565-3030
Montreal (514) 844-3318
Halifax (902) 420-1404
Newfoundland (709) 722-0430

Canadian Actor's Equity Association (CLC)
Association canadienne des artistes de la scène (CTC)
44 Victory St., 12th Fl., Toronto, ON M5C 3C4
(416) 867-9165

A good book to read if you're thinking of acting in Toronto is *Actors Guide to Agencies in Toronto*, which details 95 agencies plus more information. It's available at Theatrebooks, (416) 922-7175.

The Acting and Modelling Information Service (416-977-3832) will help you find addresses for reputable agents and provide you with additional information. The line is currently staffed by volunteers and they can't afford an 800 number, so if you're calling from out of town, or out of province, leave your phone number and they'll call you back collect.

## Stand-Up Comedian

**Age:** 17, though some comedy clubs may want you to be of age
**Pay:** *Small clubs:* nothing to a couple hundred for a few shows a week. *Larger clubs:* may pay a headliner $1000 to $10,000, depending on talent and popularity.
**Dress Code:** Depends on your act
**Job Prospects:** Good Luck
**What to Expect:** Most comics have day jobs, and make their way to the top by slugging it out at the bottom. You may need to spend several months or more doing free sessions on Open Mike Night before the club hires you to play Tuesday nights for nothing.
**What's Expected of You:** To be funny. The audience, the club owner, your fellow comedians . . . you're going to feel the pressure to be "on." As well, you'll have to conform to the standards of the club, which may mean having no standards at all.

I once got a great tip from a comic I met in Montreal. She said that when she decided to try being a comedian, she gave herself a year in which she wouldn't ask herself if she was any good. When she started, she couldn't even look the audience in the eye, she'd just stare at the floor for her whole set. By the time I saw her, she was letting it rip and the audience loved her. She just gave herself the space to be bad at it for a while, until she figured out what she was doing. That could go for most jobs, but especially this one.

**Required Knowledge Skills:** Since you can't learn how to be a comedian through any formal training, the best things to do are to write lots of material, practise lots of material, and watch a lot of different comedians work. Then find your own style.

**Where to Get Started:** The most recognized club in Canada is Yuk Yuk's, which normally has an Open Mike Night on Mondays. There are often fifteen spots available, but there are eight or so regulars who always get spots so you'll be battling for the few left open. Stick with it. Call other local comedy night clubs, or spaces where you've seen comedy performers, and ask what it takes to perform there.

You can also practise getting your creative spontaneity going by joining an improv group (or starting one of your own).

## Disc Jockey

**Age:** 15 (at parties)

**Pay:** By the job or by the hour, DJs can make anywhere from $100 to $1000 per event. A DJ charging $1000 per event can work two nights a month and spend the whole month looking for two clients, or another DJ may get $50 a night working six nights a week in a nightclub.

**Dress Code:** Depends on the club, the event, and the style of music

**Job Prospects:** With sufficient self-promotion, Fair to Good

**What to Expect:** Club DJs have the ultimate in crazy, fun jobs. And they get lots of stuff: guest list power, free drinks and T-shirts, and lots of attention. Part of that attention will be endless requests for songs you don't want to play, plan on playing later, or know will kill the dance floor in three seconds flat. People will also want your attention at crucial points when you're getting set up and under stress. Another DJ bummer is creating a wicked set and then waiting and waiting and waiting for people to show up so that you can start it. The biggest DJ pitfall is hearing the same song about a million times. It's going to happen so don't get into this unless you love music.

A DJ who you might get for a wedding or a formal might also be a club DJ in the making. However, in this case the event is the star, and expect that very few people will get it if you play a pulsating rave tune . . . they're crying out for "Old Time Rock 'n' Roll" and "Macarena."

**What's Expected of You:** In any and every case, your job is to keep people on the floor and having a great time. You've got to keep it smooth between song changes, and if you're mixing it has to make sense and sound good. Clubs will ask you not to do anything too crazy, although over time, when the owners come to trust you, you'll probably have more licence to try new sounds.

**Required Knowledge Skills:** To be obsessed by music. You already buy records of everything, and spend all your money doing so, but now you have to practise spinning records. You want to know what to play, what it'll do to the people listening, and when to play it. Further, you'll need to find out how to mix music smoothly, and to start creating your own particular sound and style. Once you've got that handled you'll need to get hooked up doing parties, and that will be for free at first.

Get business cards made and start networking. Make a demo tape to audition with at clubs. All DJs in the making should pay attention to which songs go with which people. Go out and observe. Ask other DJs. There's so much to learn about this job and the music.

**Where to Get Started:** As an independant DJ you're going to have to train yourself, buy your own music, and get yourself hooked up to the scene with a lot of persistence. Staying independent really means that you can create your own style and approach this job artistically. It's a huge commitment, and once you've invested in all those records you'll need to continue working in this field just to make it worthwhile.

If you're more interested in just having a job as a CD-playing DJ at parties, that's okay too. There are more options for you to get hired, get a contract, and get working immediately. Check out the Yellow Pages under Disc Jockey. There should be several companies listed that you could approach. If you want to find out how reputable they are, check with:

The Canadian Disc Jockey Association and National Training Advisory Council
3148 Kingston Road, Suite 202-300, Scarborough , ON M1M 1P4
(416) 755-3898

# Modelling

**Age:** 13 (as soon as you're ready both inside and out)
**Pay:** Depends on the company, the deal, and the length of the shoot, but let's just say it's very good
**Dress Code:** Very fashionable, that suits you and the season.
**Job Prospects:** Good if you've got "the look"
**What to Expect:** This is one of those random jobs that could be a source of endless frustration, a quiet series of jobs that pay well but don't really morph into a career, or a mind-blowing rise to the top (the last being the least likely but you already knew that, right?).

Most people start in modelling in one of a few ways. Either you're "discovered," you win a contest, or you actively pursue meetings with agents. If you choose the latter, be warned: a reputable agency would never have you take a course, pay for classes, or pay agent fees outside of your commissions. You may need to have test shots done, but if you're good, photographers may do it for free in order to work with you.

Just so you're clear on this, you alone will be responsible for your career, which is part of the reason why I suggest that you wait until you're really ready to undertake the job. You'll be responsible for your own development and your own finances. It's you who'll decide what jobs will be good for your overall career, and it's you who has to know that all your makeup, clothing, hair care, and so on is all tax deductible.

**What's Expected of You:** You'll have to buy a lot of clothes, shoes, and accessories, because photo shoots can't fit you for everything. Be prepared to pack four pairs of shoes, nylons, body suits, and so on for each shoot you attend. You've got to take on a lot of the responsibility for looking good. You'll need a professional attitude and tons of patience.

**Required Knowledge Skills:** How to apply makeup. How to generate attitude for the camera when you've been sitting for three hours waiting for them to light the set. How to generate attitude for when you're famous and you have to look bored all the time, even when being worshipped by most of the Western world.

**Where to Get Started:** Since being discovered isn't something you can plan, you can either enter some contests or get yourself an agent. The Acting and Modelling Information Service (416-977-3832) will help you find addresses for reputable agents and provide you with additional information. As I mentioned in the Acting section, the line is currently staffed by volunteers and can't afford an 800 number, so if you're calling from out of town, or out of province, leave your phone number and they'll call you back collect. Otherwise look up agents in your phone book. Ask around. Get advice and the best word on the good agents. Also get yourself a portfolio of photos going that you can show around. If you can get any level of photographer to take your picture, even better.

# Journalism

**Age:** 16/17 to start interning
**Pay:** Expect to start at nothing or travel fare only; as you get more experienced you may get an increase to anywhere from $100 to $400 a week, depending on what you're doing
**Dress Code:** Office wear with style (fashion magazines), or office wear with casual, artsy overtones (offbeat magazines and print publications), or office wear (conservative papers, large companies); guys tend not to have to wear ties, but definitely not jeans
**Job Prospects:** Fair to Good Luck, depending on your connections
**What to Expect:** So you're envisioning yourself as the next Woodward and Bernstein (maybe they can get Brad Pitt to play you in the movie), or maybe you've decided to become a feature columnist read by more people than Ann Landers. Whatever the angle, you've got to work your way to the top.

In order to do the working your way thing, you've got to be prepared to spend some summers doing jobs as obscure as packing shoes for photo shoots or researching speed boat races in Miami. It may not have anything to do with that burning, insightful piece on heroin addiction you've been dreaming about, but it'll give you connections, experience, and exposure. You may also be doing such unglamorous tasks as answering phones and transcribing taped interviews that someone else has written.

Eventually this will pay off, and you'll be entrusted with small pieces that appear as fillers or picture text. Then will come the leap from intern to staff or freelance writer, when you're actually writing text and proposing ideas.

**What's Expected of You:** Pitch in to do what's necessary to put the paper or issue to bed. Read the papers every day and be up on what's happening everywhere. Popular culture should be your religion.

**Required Knowledge Skills:** The ability to find information (where would you call to find out the kind of shoes Madonna wore in the early eighties?). Not being afraid of cold calls, because you'll have to call lots of people. Lots of ideas. Every paper or magazine is searching for new stories or old stories with new angles. If you're brimming with vision for hot stories, you'll be an editor's godsend.

**Where to Get Started:** First of all, get working on your school newspaper; if there isn't one start one. You need to get as much practice in as possible. Keep everything you've written, since you'll need it for your portfolio. This doesn't mean your essays from grade seven, but it does mean anything published or in the same style or subject area of the paper or magazine you're targeting.

The next step out are local community papers—free papers that cities and municipalities hand out that are less difficult to break into than the biggies. Ring up the larger papers in your area and see what internships they offer. It's true that you're better off if you have any sort of connections. If you don't, you'll have to generate some yourself. Find out where the writers hang out (hint—somewhere near the building where they work). Go to book signings or events that have to do with journalism. Talk about your passion. Offer to write on spec (for free until they know how you write) for the youth pages of your local paper. Write a short letter to some section heads proposing some ideas. Call them up and ask them the best way to get started. That's how you begin to generate your own connections.

For more information:

The Canadian Association of Journalists
Carleton University, St. Patrick's Building, Ottawa, ON K1S 5B6

Canadian Daily Newspaper Association
890 Yonge Street, Suite 110, Toronto, ON M4W 3P4

Canadian Community Newspapers Association
90 Eglinton Avenue, Toronto, ON

# WORKING WITH BIG PEOPLE (THE GOVERNMENT)

*"I learned a lot. It was pretty scientific stuff, but they were really good at making it educational."*

***—Olivia (research assistant, Environmental Core)***

*"The best part was attaining a goal by pushing yourself to where you never thought you'd go before."*

***—Sandra (army reserves)***

*"It was really inefficient, a lot of red tape. They check your work at each step. It's a good place to start working, but not a place to take initiative. It takes a long time to see the results of a project, but I recently read that 1.5 million people will be saved from skin cancer in the twenty-first century as a result of a project that I worked on."*

***—Swin (project assistant, Ministry of the Environment)***

**What to Expect:** I'm changing the format here because, the government being the government, discovering and applying for these jobs is often more difficult than the jobs themselves.

The government, at all levels, is committed to bringing jobs and training to students. Unfortunately for us, for now anyway, that commitment gets muddied by changes in offices, appointments, addresses, and names. I encourage you to seek out what the government has to offer. Be persistent. Make a lot of phone calls until you're speaking to the right person in the right department. Get hold of the addresses you need to make a proper application. Befriend the weary staff members and get them onside to your desire to work in your field of interest.

The government offers programs of richness and variety. You can work as a Park Ranger (look under Working with Nature for more information), as a Reserve Army member, as a potential member of the RCMP, in some capacity in another country such as Germany, Australia, or the Netherlands, or helping other students find jobs. The government even offers programs that provide money and resources to hook you up to these jobs. Many jobs, particularly the volunteer ones, are available year-round, but many get filled by January and February.

The key is figuring out which job links to which municipal, provincial, and federal department, and where to go to get the right information and addresses. I know this whole deal may seem like a pain in your summer employment pants, but if you're interested in something very specific and government-oriented, you may as well start dealing with these guys and gals now because it doesn't get any easier as time goes by. I think they mean to be accessible, they just don't know how. I still think that the best route is through employment centres. Counsellors there are trained to understand the mystery that surrounds government departments, offices, and ministries.

**Where to Get Started:** As I mentioned in Part 1, there are Human Resource Centres for Youth, and if you go there they can help you. That being said, many of the interesting programs require application between November and March, two to six months before the Youth Employment Centres open.

So if you're reading this sometime before March you're going to have to do your own digging, beginning with the adult employment centres. Find a counsellor and explain that you need whatever addresses and information that's available on whatever program you're interested in or on what programs the government offers. If they don't have it, be persistent and ask who does. You may have to go to the local office of your provincial or municipal ministry to find the information.

### Federal Addresses

(For other offices, look under Government of Canada in the blue pages of your local telephone directory.)

### Human Resources Development Canada

Specialized Youth Unit
2131 Lawrence Ave. East, Toronto, ON
(416) 752-5522

### FSSEP: The Federal Summer Student Employment Program

This particular program requires you to fill out a standard application form that's put into a pool for government agencies to check out. This application form may have you wondering if the government truly knows the meaning of simplicity (answer: no), but persevere, for if you can mark the correct codes in the proper pen colour (black or very dark blue), you'll make it possible to hook up to the Canada Employment Centres for Students Program, the Native Internship Program, the Defence Research Assistant Program, the Geological Survey of Canada Student Assistants Program, the Law Program, the Audit Trainee Program, the Summer Student Employment at Vimy, France, the Student Customs Officer Program (there's a power trip!), the Inshore Rescue Boat Program, and the Aboriginal Summer Student Employment Training (ASSET).

Each of these programs has requirements, the most basic for all being that you're the minimum age to work in the province where the job exists, that you're currently enrolled as a full-time student, and that you'll still be enrolled in the fall. If you're not a Canadian citizen but you're studying here, you can roll the dice and give it a try. Preference will be given to Canadian citizens.

If you've tried the government route before, this program now replaces the old COSEP (Career Oriented Student Employment Program) and non-COSEP programs. Remember how I mentioned governmental name changes? That's why it's crucial not to take my word for it, but to take responsibility for tracking this information down yourself.

### Volunteers Program (Federal)

If you have an interest in science and are at least seventeen years old you can investigate this program, which links you up with earth scientists, technologists, and other professionals to do hands-on assignments. Students can assist in the lab, the field, the library, or other varied environments. This program runs throughout the year, depending on the assignment.

Volunteers Program Coordinator
Geological Survey of Canada
Natural Resources Canada
601 Booth Street, Rm. 205, Ottawa, ON K1A 0E4
(613) 992-7362

### Summer Career Placements (Federal)

Are you a senior high school, college, or university student who wants experience in your field but is having trouble getting hired because the organizations have no money? The government does provide wage subsidies to not-for-profit organizations and private sector businesses so that they can create career-related summer jobs for students that last eight to sixteen weeks. Basically, funding is available for employers who couldn't otherwise hire you. So if you know of some place that's eager to take you on and train you in some capacity, then you can get an application (available by the end of February) at the Canada Employment Centres. This process of creating a proposal may seem like a logistical nightmare, but if you're committed to learning some skills and working in a place that wouldn't normally be able to pay you, go for it.

### Environmental Youth Core

The EYC is set up for the advancement of environmental protection in Canada. Eligible employers are non-governmental organizations involved in environmental awareness and resource protection, conservation, and enhancement activities; public interest and environmental advocacy groups; local tourist associations; Aboriginal groups and band councils; conservation authorities; school boards;

universities and colleges; and muncipalities. The ministries won't hire you, but they'll direct you to employers who can.
**Age:** 15 to 24 (or 15 to 29 if disabled)
**Timing:** Year-round
**Check:**

Ministry of Agriculture and Food
Ministry of Culture, Tourism and Recreation
Ministry of Environment and Energy
Ministry of Natural Resources
Ministry of Northern Development and Mines

# Reserves (Canadian Armed Forces)

**Age:** 17 (16 if your birthday is in July)
**Pay:** On average $62 a day (over 6 hours); $31 a day (under 6 hours); around $3500 for a 6 to 8-week stretch full-time
**Dress Code:** One of three uniforms
**Job Prospects:** Excellent if you pass the initial tests
**What to Expect:** If you think your household is regimented, try joining the army for the summer. Once you fulfill the requirements of a grade ten education (at the minimum), an aptitude test, a medical test, an interview, and a phys. ed. test, you can choose from a variety of jobs. The Reserves don't hire on a first-come first-served basis, but rather according to a merit list of how well you did on all those entrance tests. From there you can choose from a long list of interesting jobs, including infantry, naval, tank driver, weapons technology, medical support, finance, administration, and fifty others.

If you're a landed immigrant you can also join the Reserves. There's no contract; the reserves are strictly voluntary. That means no one will be shipping you off to some unknown overseas crisis when all you wanted was a summer job with room and board. The only catch is that you're committing to year-round employment. During the school year you work one night a week and one weekend a month (for which, of course, you get paid).

The Reserves aren't for everyone. You have to be energetic, because you'll be working long hours and in many instances doing a lot of physical training and labour. The company you work for is the army, so expect discipline, lots of structure, and the usual amount of bureaucratic stuff that accompanies any government-regulated, hierarchical-type job. The worst of the Reserves is probably that it can get stifling, with little free thought involved. The best parts will be working with other young people and students, working hard and seeing something through, and getting the satisfaction that comes from completing a project or learning a skill.

**What's Expected of You:** Discipline, dedication, the ability to follow orders, and lots of energy.

**Required Knowledge Skills:** Once you've passed the basic entrance tests, the Reserves will be a place of learning for you.

**Where to Get Started:** Head for your nearest Canadian Forces Recruiting Centre, or ask at your Youth Employment Centre, which will probably have a posting for the Reserves already up.

# WORKING WITH CUSTOMERS AND POTENTIAL CUSTOMERS

*"There's an allure to the [comic book] store . . . but it's not a party or a dream job like I thought . . . it's hard work and you get tired at the end of the day. It's a retail job, it's stock and it's merchandise like anything else . . . but I find liking comics helps in talking to customers when they want to know what's coming in."*

***—Jacques (retail)***

*"I worked in a second-hand shop for mothers and children. I was the only one in the store, but at least I had a nice, quiet place to do my homework."*

***—Valerie (retail)***

*"Sometimes I took it personally when a door was slammed in my face, but it helped that I believed in [Earthroots]. . . . After a while at the job I felt like I could do anything. I mean I was convincing people to give me money."*

***—Christine (door-to-door sales for an environmental group)***

*"Tours are the one job where you can get paid amazing money and have ninety percent of the people love you more than their own grandchild. This is an incredibly ego-focused job, and incredibly hard work."*

***—Bruce (tour escort)***

## Retail

**Age:** 15/16
**Pay:** Minimum, with small wage increases based on length of time working; commissions, incentives, or discounts might be included
**Dress Code:** Varies from store to store (usually casual but neat attire)
**Job Prospects:** Excellent
**What to Expect:** Whether you're working in a clothing shop, a video store, or Lucy's Kitchen Cutlery Cabaret, working retail is the same all over. Your job, should you choose to accept it, is to bend over backwards to help customers find what they need and get what they want. Although your feet may ache, and you never want to search through a pile for a size 12 narrow classic fit again, if the customer asks, you'll jump to fulfill their desires.
**What's Expected of You:** Your constant focus on the job at hand: who needs help, who needs attention, and if there are no customers, what administrative or functional tasks need to be done to keep the store in working order.
**Required Knowledge Skills:** How to fold neatly (if you work in a clothing store, be prepared to fold a lot), and how to work a cash register (or learn on the job).
**Where to Get Started:** The key is to find the type of service (clothes, food, books, videos, computers) that you're already comfortable with, and then you'll know which stores to approach. Re-read the Pounding the Pavement section in Chapter 5 for how to best approach the managers and owners of these establishments. Ask yourself: "Lots of people want a job—why do I want a job in this particular store?" This will do a lot for how you approach these stores, and for your commitment to working there.

## Gas Station Attendant

**Age:** 18/19 (could be younger if the station doesn't sell cigarettes)
**Pay:** Minimum wage and a bit above
**Dress Code:** Coveralls or provided work shirt

**Job Prospects:** Good
**What to Expect:** If the station is self-serve you'll be the commander of the booth, but if you work at a full-service gas station a lot more service is required. Not only do you have to pump gas, wipe windshields, and check oil, your customer service skills will be more in demand since you'll be interacting with people who've decided to pay more money so that you can do it for them. This job could be a great opener to getting a job as a mechanic, particularly if the station you work for has a garage. Still, pumping gas on rainy nights and running inside to make change for a fifty may not be as comfortable as that bulletproof booth.
**What's Expected of You:** Basic cash handling.
**Required Knowledge Skills:** How to wipe a windshield at high speed without breaking the wipers.
**Where to Get Started:** This kind of job may require you to approach all your local gas stations. If you drive a car, or have access to your family car, do you go somewhere regularly where they already know you? Can they get to know you? Re-read Chapter 5's Pounding the Pavement section.

# Bank Teller

**Age:** 17 at the youngest, more likely 18
**Pay:** $8 to $11 an hour
**Dress Code:** Conservative office attire
**Job Prospects:** Good
**What to Expect:** For the most part, you'll be doing deposits, withdrawals, transfers, credit card and utility payments, as well as updating the passbooks of people like me who go to the bank once a month and have three pages of computer data to enter into their passbook.

This particular form of working with customers requires more than just a head for numbers. Money is a sensitive issue for 99.9 percent of the people on this planet, so you're dealing with people's lives when you deal with their cash. This means that as well as handling the routine customer transactions you're going to see some stressed-out, pissed-off, frightened people.
**What's Expected of You:** With high competition between banks and trust companies these days, you're the customer service conduit to client satisfaction and repeat

business. You're going to be trusted to make few mistakes and at the same time pay attention to the clients' needs. As well, due to the large sums of money that you'll handle every day, honesty and integrity will be the number one values that banks are expecting from you.

**Required Knowledge Skills:** Obviously, strong math skills are a plus. Even if counting stacks of fifties is your dream job, you'll also need to know how to make change and convert numbers quickly (your mental math skills will skyrocket). You'll need to be detail-oriented and have decent problem-solving skills in order to determine where a mistake has been made. Then you'll need diplomacy to handle the resulting furor.

**Where to Get Started:** There are so many banks and trust companies, and the good news is that most have summer and part-time positions available and encourage your application. For summer work, some banks like Toronto-Dominion want your application in January and February, while Citibank said April or May would be fine. Different banks run on different schedules, so don't assume that if the doors are closed at one bank they're closed by all.

Most of the banks that I (meaning my wonderful researcher Nicole) talked to said to mail in your résumé and cover letter, except for Canada Trustco Mortgage Co., which so smartly requested them in person. I still say that it can't hurt to go to your local branch, make an appointment with the branch manager, and ask about their jobs. They're into servicing the community and that's you. Then if they still want you to mail in your résumé, you can address it directly to the person who you met so that he or she will know who you are. A guy I know who works higher up in the bank also mentioned that if you're stopping by (he thought that was a good idea too), think about dressing appropriately. Review Chapters 5 and 6 for further suggestions.

If you're fluent in Greek, Italian, Portuguese, Spanish, or any of the Asian languages, find the banks in areas that will welcome that valuable employee asset.

For more information on this field in general, you can contact the Canadian Bankers' Association, which puts out pamphlets and publications on careers in banking.

The Canadian Bankers' Association
Commerce Court West, 30th Fl.
P.O. Box 348
Toronto, ON M5L 1G2
(416) 362-6092

# Door-to-Door Sales

**Age:** 16 (could be younger, but go in pairs for safety's sake)
**Pay:** Commission
**Dress Code:** Something trustworthy and non-threatening
**Job Prospects:** Good
**What to Expect:** Rejection. Lots and lots of rejection. And the amount of rejection will depend on what's being sold. Now, that being said, I believe that no one can really reject you; they can can only refuse what you have to offer. The difference is subtle but powerful. And if you're selling something you believe in, it'll be easier to stay committed to this job.

Door-to-door jobs range from free estimate appointments for painting, roofing, or repair companies to selling specific products like ink stamps or knife sets to households or merchants. Again, this kind of selling takes patience, persistence, and a thick skin. As you get used to your "rap" or "spiel," it becomes easier to approach people with it and to answer their questions.
**What's Expected of You:** The ability to pick yourself up, dust off the refusals, and go again.
**Required Knowledge Skills:** How to get people to open the door. How to avoid getting your face caught in a shutting door.
**Where to Get Started:** Door-to-door jobs are easy to get because so many people find them difficult. Charities are always looking for people to champion their cause. This job is one of those that you'll probably find most often from newspaper ads, so I recommend looking there first.

# Telemarketing Sales

**Age:** 15/16
**Pay:** Minimum wage and a bit above, or by commission
**Dress Code:** They can't see you on the phone, but look decent so that you don't scare your employer.

**Job Prospects:** Excellent

**What to Expect:** This job can be either halfway decent or absolute hell. The best part about it is that most places will hire anyone, regardless of past experiences, as long as the applicant looks interested and is somewhat articulate. That means getting a job and a steady pay cheque if you can handle all the other garbage that comes with this job.

If you're doing telephone sales, quotas have to be filled and you'll face constant rejection. Beware of telemarketing ads that are carried week after week. A repeat want ad means that either the employers are having trouble keeping people in the job or that they're firing everyone after each training session in order to keep their benefit packages.

On the good side, there are excellent tele-researching jobs. These are harder to find, but you'll be involved in market research instead of selling. People tend to treat you much better on the other end of the phone when you're asking for their opinions instead of their money. Some people will actually discuss mayonnaise for forty-five minutes.

The variances in work environments can make a huge difference. Some places won't let you get up and stretch and instead make you keep dialing. Try to choose a work environment that will let you take a bathroom break. Also beware of too-good offers, such as 100 percent commissions and promises of bonuses. These places usually set high, often unreachable quotas to fill before you ever see any bonus money.

**What's Expected of You:** In the face of consistent refusals, the same cheerful "try, try again" attitude that door-to-door demands.

**Required Knowledge Skills:** Speaking clearly and sounding like a person, not a creep.

**Where to Get Started:** Finding a good telemarketing job is a bit like Russian roulette. Some places will want you to lie about free gifts to make a sale. Good telemarketing jobs are to be found with charity work and school donations (if you're in university, your campus will probably have jobs available), and with market research. If they're lying to you up front, the job is probably a stinker. It's important to find out right away *what* you'll be selling—donations, estimates, products, a service—and *how* exactly you'll be making your money.

As with door-to-door sales, lots of telemarketing jobs get advertised in the newspaper. You can also try your school, or a marketing research company.

# Hotel Services (front desk clerk, bellhop)

**Age:** 17/18
**Pay:** Minimum wage and a bit above
**Dress Code:** The hotel uniform
**Job Prospects:** Good
**What to Expect:** Hotels come with their own bonuses. Often hotels will provide their staff with free meals, and even better, hotel rooms around the world at cost. Meaning that you could travel anywhere and get a posh suite for fifteen bucks a night. Wow, you say? What do I have to do for that? I'll tell you.

*Bellhop:* The aim of the bellhop is to help the guests anyway he or she can. Now obviously, this means bringing luggage up to the rooms, which requires a fair amount of physical labour (though hopefully you'll get one of those neat carts), hailing taxis and calling buses, holding things for guests on the go, providing information to a guest who's looking for quick directions, and doing some security work in the form of patrolling the hotel, particularly at night. The bellhop may even be asked to drive the shuttle to the airport, or stop someone making off with most of the mini bar, if that's what's necessary.

*Front Desk Clerk:* The front trenches of hotel work. Again, service is the main priority. You'll find yourself checking guests in and out, making reservations, running the switchboard, answering questions, and working out people's convoluted bills. Be prepared for frazzled travellers who don't like waiting and aren't going to be happy to discover that you have no record of their reservation. You'll have to be polite in the face of adversity and grumpiness. You may work weird shifts, like 7 a.m. to 4 p.m., or all night until 6 a.m. You'll probably have to learn a very specific computer system that's been created for the hotel.
**What's Expected of You:** Exemplary service, a polite and cheerful demeanour, and a willingness to go out of your way for a customer. I still remember a hotel clerk named Vito in Chicago who got me into his hotel despite a million conventions, because I was slowly dying from heat and cockroach exposure in a youth hostel. Let me tell you, the Executive Plaza was my hotel of choice from then on. If you can inspire that kind of loyalty from customers, you'll be a gift to any hotel manager.
**Required Knowledge Skills:** To smile in the face of adversity.
**Where to Get Started:** You can go to each hotel to apply directly for an interview, or you can keep an eye out in newspapers and on job boards, because these are often jobs that get advertised, particularly for chain hotels.

# Tour Guide

**Age:** 16/17
**Pay:** Around $70 per day, depending on the place and the company
**Dress Code:** Most likely a jacket and tie type uniform
**Job Prospects:** Good (particularly since this is often seasonal summer work)
**What to Expect:** Because there are so many versions of the tour guide you could get this kind of job in many areas. There are tours of your city, or trip tours going outside your city to places like Whistler or Niagara Falls. You could lead tours around your school campus or a historical site (from the Rockies to Pioneer Village). You could be dressing up in old soldier costumes and dramatizing history, or you could be just chatting away about the chronicles of a local historical site or museum.

Remember that the tour groups you lead are looking to you, not only to provide information about what they're seeing, but also to make the landscape or the narrative come alive with your telling. They want to picture what it was really like in the eighteenth century, or what it would be like to drop down the Falls in a barrel. You're their access to remembering something interesting from their trip or visit. You're going to be looked upon as a leader, as someone with knowledge, so you can expect to be treated with some respect. On the other hand, you'll also be treated with some boredom by those who were dragged to the museum, or by people who've been on their feet all day. You can't take it personally; you just have to keep plugging away at that Canadian history.
**What's Expected of You:** Without question, enthusiasm is number one, and being hot to trot out all the info regarding the tour at hand.
**Required Knowledge Skills:** Although your spiel will be taught to you by those who hire you, it may also be handy to have another language or two.
**Where to Get Started:** First you have to decide what kind of tour you'd be interested in leading. If you don't mind being indoors, maybe a museum or historical site would be for you. These are often more toned down, with little pageantry, and are more informative than dramatic. You'd apply directly to the site for these jobs. If you like a little more speech-making and friendly chatting, leading a city tour or local trip tours may be more your style. You could do this on a boat, a bus, or on foot. Look under Sightseeing Tours in the Yellow Pages as a place to start. If you're from a

particular background or speak another language fluently, see if there are tours that cater to this group specifically, because you'd be a tremendous asset to the company. Finally, there are the ultimate in dramatic jobs, wherein you can be a eighteenth century soldier, *coureur du bois*, or candlemaker. The tours you lead could be more focused on activities or on re-enacting history. You'll have to investigate local sites where these are conducted. Finally, you may want to investigate nature or walking tours. Places that have these kind of tours include conservatories, public gardens, and parks; you'll have to investigate each of these separately. Go to the local tourist information bureau to find out what's available in your city or town. For the phone numbers of your provincial tourism bureau (to get brochures that'll have lots of tourism ideas), flip to the Regional Events section of this book.

## Tour Escort

**Age:** 19
**Pay:** $100/150 per day
**Dress Code:** Presentable khakis and cotton wear by day; tuxedos and good dresses for possible formal occasions
**Job Prospects:** Good Luck
**What to Expect:** The difference between this job and a regular tour guide is the amount of travel and time you'll have to put into it. A tour escort is someone who'll take a tour group from Canada to the great wineries of France, or on a cruise ship on the Baltic Sea, or on a round trip of Europe's great cities, or even on tours of New York City. Of course this means you'll be away from home for a week to a month at a time, and during that time you must be prepared to give yourself over to the group. If you thought that being a tour guide would sap your energy, you'd better not even consider being a tour escort, because it requires excitement, enthusiasm, and eternal devotion: in short, it's a 24-hour job.

Your group will bond with you. If they're fifteen-year-olds they'll have crushes on you, and if they're eighty-year-olds they'll tell you about their families back home. All kinds of dramas will occur and all the variations of group dynamics will have to be managed by you. It'll be your job to keep the group safe, entertained, informed, and satisfied with their journey.

You can expect lots of attention, and maybe even some unwanted attention, as you turn therapist or mediator to members of your party. There may be occasions when you'll have to recognize someone's birthday in a special way, or go out of your way to help someone buy the perfect souvenir from their visit. Although you'll get a lot of recognition and feedback, you'll also have to devote much of your time and energy to your group.

**What's Expected of You:** Some life and travel experience, a lot of enthusiasm and leadership, maturity, and a prize-winning personality.

**Required Knowledge Skills:** Languages are a help, but not as big a concern as with the tour guide jobs. You'll be taught what you need to say to your group, but any additional understanding of the area or the country would be excellent.

**Where to Get Started:** Although not an easy field to break into, there are plenty of travel companies The first thing to do is go to a couple of travel agents and get every brochure that refers to a tour. This is the last job interview you want to rein it in on. That doesn't mean shouting facts about the Nile at your interviewer, but it does mean demonstrating the ways in which you can be articulate and knowledgeable, as well as being passionate about travelling.

# WORKING WITH FOOD

*"Every person should have to serve in the service industry to understand how stressful it gets. But anybody can learn how to do it."*
***—Kim (waiting tables)***

*"It's a wired job, very intense . . . it's more fun than I expected—definitely a rollercoaster ride."*
***—Hagar (waiting tables)***

*"I worked one day dishwashing and shredding chickens in a restaurant kitchen. It was slimy, greasy, and gross."*
***—Jay (kitchen job)***

*"I learned not to take s—t . . . and how to do it delicately."*
***—Martha (bartending)***

*"Where's Potpan that he helps not to take away?"*
***—William Shakespeare***

# Wait Staff

**Age:** 14 minimum, 19 (or your province's age limit) to serve alcohol
**Pay:** Usually minimum, plus tips
**Dress Code:** Whatever the restaurant wishes
**Job Prospects:** Excellent
**What to Expect:** Your first table wants to hear all the specials a second time, table 3 wants their coffees different ways, table 6 wants to give you a lecture on which herbal teas actually contain caffeine, and table 2 can't string a sentence together but think it's a good time to have another. Whether you're waiting tables at a greasy spoon or at a high class restaurant, the duties are pretty much the same. Approach customers, take their order, deliver the order to the kitchen, and when the food is ready take it out. Present the bill, and voilà! you're a waiter. It all sounds pretty simple until you take off your shoes and count the blisters.

Like tree planting, you have to be in it for the money—not the below-minimum wage amount that appears on every cheque, but the tips. The beauty of tips is instant cash. Patrons of lower-scale diners and cafés leave smaller tips, but the turnover at the tables is higher, hence more chances to be tipped. In expensive restaurants, the turnover may only happen twice on a dinner shift, or in some cases not at all. But the bill will be much higher, so your standard 10 to 15 percent could be $100 a table.

**What's Expected of You:** You're the mover and shaker who gets the right food orders to the right tables before starving customers rise up against the kitchen staff. Even when you're incredibly stressed and tired, you're still expected to be nice to customers.

**Required Knowledge Skills:** To be able to remember at least six mental items while doing at least seven physical tasks. You should know how to make change, what the Shepherd's Pie's like, and whether the salad can be served as a half order.

**Where to Get Started:** Do you know someone who owns or manages a restaurant? They might be able to get you a job right off the bat, even if it's just busing; that is, clearing tables, filling water glasses, etc. If they can't offer you a job, maybe they'd be willing to let you hang around the restaurant while they show you the ropes, or even let you work for a day or two. Then you can approach another restaurant with "experience."

If you have a favourite restaurant where you always eat and the staff and managers recognize you, approach them about the possibility of working there. Another idea is to start low on the totem pole, at behind-the-counter service at doughnut shops, sandwich places, or coffee chains. That way you can get the feel of taking orders and making change. With a good résumé, that should be enough to prove to any decent restaurant that you can handle the fast pace of table service.

Most students find they get restaurant jobs because they know someone else working on the staff of a restaurant who tells them when there's a shift or job opening and is willing to vouch for their friend's abilities. Often a manager doesn't want to go through the long and tedious process of hiring and would prefer to get someone to cover tomorrow's evening shift TODAY. Even if you go door to door offering your services to restaurants in person, you'll quite likely hit on a place that needs someone to fill in immediately.

## Bartending

**Age:** 18 (19 where the drinking age is such)
**Pay:** $5.95 to $8 an hour, plus tips (can work out to $15 to $20 an hour)
**Dress Code:** Depending on the bar, cool grunge wear
**Job Prospects:** Good, once you know what you're mixing
**What to Expect:** Dealing with weirdos, nice people, and people trying to pick you up. Once a bar gets into full swing there'll be no time to pull moves like Tom Cruise did in the movie *Cocktail,* i.e. spin bottles in the air and jump on the counter to recite bad poetry. A good bartender knows when to assess that, although there are five beers left in the fridge, now is the time to replace the stock, not twenty minutes later when ten people want that kind of beer.

A social person can be really happy in this job, even though the best shifts tipwise are also the nights that everyone else goes out. You may be giving up the best of your weekends, but while everyone else gets to flirt, get loaded, and go home with someone, you're sober, keeping the winks to a minimum, and walking home with cash in your pocket.
**What's Expected of You:** Serve, serve, serve.

**Required Knowledge Skills:** How to mix drinks. There are bartending schools, and you can also see if a bartending class is offered at your local college, usually under Hospitality courses.

The Bartending School of Ontario
744 Broadview Ave., Toronto, ON M4K 2P1
(416) 466-7847

**Where to Get Started:** As with restaurants, any potential bartender should assess the working environment in which he or she will function best. If you'd like to work with students and others of your age and stage, there are campus bars and bars in student-populated areas that cater to students only. If you want a more mixed crowd, look for a larger bar that attracts a cross-section of people, maybe at different times during the week.

You'll need to do a lot of cold calling, or better, walking in off the street and chatting up bar owners. Friends can really help you get hired, so look to your connections, even with people who attend bars frequently enough to know the owners.

# Busing

**Age:** 14
**Pay:** Minimum wage (sometimes shared tips)
**Dress Code:** White apron or whatever the restaurant wants
**Job Prospects:** Good to Excellent
**What to Expect:** For the most part you're dealing with people's waste. You're clearing their dirty plates, re-filling their water glasses, filling salt and pepper shakers, carrying trays of gunk back and forth, taking out the trash, and you're definitely mopping, sweeping, and vacuuming. Sounds like it sucks, huh?

So, yes, it may suck for the most part, but you could really get into the Zen of a job where you're not the one responsible if the meat's too tough or if the order is wrong, but you still get to race around and help keep the restaurant running. Also, you could (if you were somewhat older) bus at a club where you'd get to listen to great music and wear cooler clothes. If worse comes to worse and you hate it, it's a foot in the door to becoming a waiter, dishwasher, or cook.

**What's Expected of You:** To quickly and quietly do the things that no one has the time or the stomach to do.
**Required Knowledge Skills:** How to pour water. How to clear plates.
**Where to Get Started:** See Waiting and Bartending entries above.

## Dishwashing

**Age:** 14
**Pay:** Minimum to start, plus probable free meals
**Dress Code:** White apron or whatever the restaurant provides
**Job Prospects:** Good
**What to Expect:** If you've already read Part 1 of this book, you should have a good idea of what dishwashing is all about. If you haven't read Part 1, go back and start this book again. No, really, just check out Steve Santerini's résumé and cover letters, and you'll get the ups and downs of this job.
**What's Expected of You:** Clean dishes at a constant pace.
**Required Knowledge Skills:** Organization, prioritization, and communication.
**Where to Get Started:** Check the previous Working with Food entries.

## Hostessing

**Age:** 16
**Pay:** Minimum wage to start
**Dress Code:** Whatever the restaurant wants
**Job Prospects:** Fair
**What to Expect:** This job is usually at fine restaurants, or restaurants where there's a high turnover of customers and a lot of people have to be seated. The host or hostess is the person who arranges the seating, takes reservations, and shows customers to their seats. They also provide a sort of back up to the rest of

the staff, providing menus, maybe pouring water, and flagging an errant waiter down when customers are waiting for their bill. A host or hostess doesn't usually get tips, but on the other hand it's a bit of a saner job description. Being a host is a good place to get your foot in the "waiting" job door, as less experience is required for this meeting and greeting job.

**What's Expected of You:** The first friendly face, and the one who lends an air of elegance and sophistication or whatever attitude the restaurant is trying to present. You're there to keep things running smoothly and to make the customers feel special.

**Required Knowledge Skills:** Knowing how a restaurant functions, and what different wait staff members can handle, is very important. You'll be the one who decides who can handle the table of twenty, and who's going to get the family of seven. You have to fairly distribute the clientele among the staff.

**Where to Get Started:** See entries above.

## Fast Food/Counter Service

**Age:** 14 (some companies require a note of permission from parents)

**Pay:** Minimum wage, with possible minor wage increases over time

**Dress Code:** Most likely the store's uniform (stop whining and just wear the hat)

**Job Prospects:** Good to Excellent

**What to Expect:** Okay, we've all heard the phrase "Do you want fries with that?" The thing is that this job, despite the jokes that surround it, is a respectable and even exceptional job to get. There are several reasons for this. You'll get very well trained (particularly at the very well-known chains) in customer service, which will be invaluable in future jobs. The whole point to the question "Do you want fries with that?" is to upsell the customer into ordering more, while providing pleasant, helpful service. You'll also be trained in several aspects of the job—food preparation, customer service, cash, and cleaning—which will come in handy in the future.

**What's Expected of You:** You'll need to be trustworthy, reliable, FAST, efficient, and uncomplaining in the face of endless rush periods.

**Required Knowledge Skills:** Though no experience is really necessary, remember the story in Chapter 5 of the two students who memorized the menu at McDonald's. Knowing the restaurant well will give you an edge.
**Where to Get Started:** Most of these places have a standard application form (which is sometimes available right near the counter) and then a series of interviews. These are worth preparing for, so review Chapters 5 and 6. Since all you have to do is follow the Golden Arches or look for the bucket of chicken, I'll assume this part is a no-brainer and you can handle it. Remember to be as flexible as you can with your available hours. And don't forget mall food courts.

## Catering

**Age:** 15/16, depending on who hires you
**Pay:** $10 to $15 an hour
**Dress Code:** Whatever the occasion demands
**Job Prospects:** Fair to Good (with connections)
**What to Expect:** Whether you're hired by a catering company, restaurant, or your mother's best friend, catering is a way to try out the easy version of waitressing, get some experience, and make some money. Catering is easier because you take no orders, you just pass. The key word of the catering world is, in fact, "pass." Nobody eats at parties unless it's offered, and you're going to be pushing food on everybody.

Your feet might get sore and you might never want to look another shrimp puff in the eye, but you're going to circulate with whatever they hand you for the whole party. You might get to help prepare the food, which is fun if you have a creative bent.
**What's Expected of You:** That you keep unobtrusively and quickly passing the food on your tray.
**Required Knowledge Skills:** Wait staff experience is preferred.
**Where to Get Started:** The best way in is through connections, but in lieu of that, catering companies are listed right there in the Yellow Pages under—surprise, surprise—Caterers. Practise your cold calls and go for it. Remember that specific seasons are busier than others. For instance, the Christmas holidays are good (start approaching companies in November), and January and February are slow.

# WORKING WITH NATURE AND ATHLETICS

*"It's a love/hate thing. You're putting your hand in the earth 2500 times a day. But you have to plant through everything."*

***—Marcia (tree planting)***

*"I would say that it's 10 to 15 percent physical and the rest is in your head. You either love it or hate it and you have to convince yourself that you love it."*

***—Matt (tree planting)***

*"It was brutal."*

***—Martha (tree planting)***

*"It's the perfect job for a university student. I'd be exercising anyway, I'd only teach a short time, and it's fun."*

***—Erin Kate (aerobics instructor)***

## Tree Planting

**Age:** 17/18
**Pay:** You get paid by how much you plant, so you could get something like 8 cents a tree. Depending on whether you stick it out and how fast you plant, you could make anywhere from $2000 to $5000, with most people falling into an average of $3500 in six or seven weeks.
**Dress Code:** The same thing you wore yesterday, and the day before that.
**Job Prospects:** Fair if you're a newcomer (friend connections help a lot)
**What to Expect:** Tree planting is the grittiest, hardest, most labour-intensive jobs you'll ever have the pleasure of cramping your hands over. And, as I'm told by tree planter after tree planter, it has less to do with your state of physical fitness and more to do with the power of your mind to overcome incredibly rigorous conditions. Even "lifers" (those who plant year after year) say that the first few weeks always make them wonder what they're doing back.

Most companies require that you supply all of your work materials: tent, sleeping bag, steel-toed boots, and planting equipment.

The first three weeks are the hardest, particularly since no one talks much to each other, and everyone is so intent on getting to bed early before getting up by 5 a.m. that it feels as though you've sold your summer into worse than prison. But people will warm up, and soon it'll become a work-hard, play-hard party camp and you'll find yourself connecting with people who you never thought existed on the planet. Apparently there's nothing like a ride in a 4x4 up to your lonely piece where you'll plant by yourself for the day (or maybe with one other person), taping up your hands, and eating a cold pancake smeared with peanut butter. I myself don't understand it, but I'm told that it's an incredibly empowering experience, if you can survive it.

Also a bonus, the planting season runs from May through to the begininng of July. That's bad news for high school students, but university students can line up another job in the city for July and August, maximizing their summer work situation.

**What's Expected of You:** Come rain, come snow, come sleet, come shine, you'll plant every day and you'll make the quota set for you. You think I'm kidding? A friend of mine was diagnosed with bronchitis from planting on a mountain covered in snow. She went back and planted the next day. These people are insane.

**Required Knowledge Skills:** Pure mental stamina and a burning desire for cash.

**Where to Get Started:** It's hard to break into the tree planting world when you're a first-year planter. Friends who've planted before and can recommend you to their company are probably your best bet. There are big companies and small companies, and some have better contracts than others. Also, note that in your first year you may not make as much as you hoped. You'll spend the first three weeks figuring out how to plant, the next two weeks building up your quota, and the last two weeks working like a fiend—only to break even on those first three weeks when you made barely anything. Here are two possibilities to start with. Look for advertisements, and most importantly, talk to friends who've planted before. These companies change all the time.

Brinkman & Associates
North Bay, ON
(705) 663-1180
520 Sharpe St., New Westminster, BC V3M 4R2
(604) 521-7771

Coast Range
BC
(604) 681-2626
(604) 932-4477

# Sports Lessons

**Age:** 17 or 18
**Pay:** about $7 to $10, depending on skill level
**Dress Code:** Sports-related gear
**Job Prospects:** Good (depending on the sport)
**What to Expect:** Although this field is too full and varied to outline each and every possibility, the advantage of having a thorough knowledge of a certain sport is that other people will pay to learn it too. So whether you teach skiing, tennis, baseball, martial arts, or sailing (and so on and so on), the number one thing you can expect is to be truly immersed in the sport of your choice.

You'll probably be expected to be able to teach the concepts behind the sport, for instance sailing vectors, basketball defensive plays, and doubles strategy. Plus you may be expected to entertain your charges when it rains.
**What's Expected of You:** You need to be able to break the sport down into learnable pieces so that your beginners or novices can understand and assimilate. You'll need lesson plans, knowledge of the theory, and back-up plans. Basically, you need to develop your teaching skills.

You're also going to need the same sorts of skills you'd need to be a camp counsellor. That means an enthusiastic, energetic, outgoing personality, and the patience to deal with any type of student you might get.
**Required Knowledge Skills:** If you're already interested in a sport, find out if any particular certification is necessary to teach further down the line. Otherwise, you'll need to be an expert in the ins and outs of your particular sport. Racing or competing in the sport is also a good idea, as it provides another proof of your ability that you can use in applications and advertising.
**Where to Get Started:** Apply to local recreation centres, schools with activity programs after school and during breaks, resorts, day camps, and camps. There are also specialty camps for every conceivable sport. If you're at a camp, you could develop and head up a particular teaching program. Camps often require less certification than other places, and are a great place to get teaching experience.

# Parks and Rec

**Age:** 16
**Pay:** Minimum wage with room for wage increases
**Dress Code:** Dress for the particular recreation, or in outdoor work clothes
**Job Prospects:** Good, if you apply on time
**What to Expect:** Cleaning up the litter, pruning and mowing hedges, raking leaves and shovelling snow paths; child care; and teaching everything from yoga to skiing. Your city's Parks and Rec department looks after all the parks and green spaces and provides recreation at an affordable price.

The fall, winter, and spring hiring is often done by August, so get your application in while the sun's still shining.

**What's Expected of You:** Enthusiasm, responsibility, and care of your community and of community property.
**Required Knowledge Skills:** The park half will require less knowledge, and you can probably learn on the job. The recreation half requires some knowledge about the activity you'll be teaching, or experience with children.
**Where to Get Started:** Each city or subsection of the city distributes some kind of flyer or newspaper that outlines the services they provide. One of the best places to find these is in your local library. They're free, and list the current activities, dates, times, and even phone numbers to apply for seasonal help. If you can't find the paper, use your phone book to call Parks and Rec to offer your services. Each section may hire separately, so you'll have to be specific about what you'd like to do.

# Aerobics Instructor

**Age:** 16/17
**Pay:** Anywhere from $10 to $25 an hour (depends on the gym and the city's going rate)
**Dress Code:** Professional athletic workout wear
**Job Prospects:** Excellent, once you're trained

**What to Expect:** A good hourly wage, flexible schedule, possible free gym membership, and being paid for working out. If you have a natural enthusiasm and a love of working out, being an aerobics instructor will neatly combine these abilities.

You have to be willing to do three to six months of preparation though. You'll have to get certified, and prepare workout tapes as well as up-to-date, technically correct, and fun routines that people can safely follow. If you want more flexibility in your teaching, you'll likely need several routines—one step, one low-impact, and one mix of high- and low-impact, or some combination of these.

This job doesn't require a huge time commitment. You can show up fifteen minutes before the class starts, and hang around for five or ten minutes afterwards for questions from your clients. You can expect a lot of questions, good and bad, and you'll be looked upon as a fitness expert, so you'd better have some decent answers.

**What's Expected of You:** Students can hurt themselves, so remember that you're responsible for their bodies and well-being.

**Required Knowledge Skills:** You can get certified through your YMCA, local gym, or the Phys. Ed. department of your school. There's also an organization called CAIN (Canadian Association of Instructors Network) that you could try contacting for information on how to get qualified. Ask the instructors at your gym how they got started and where they were certified.

**Where to Get Started:** Start by working for the YMCA, Parks and Rec, or the gym at your university. You'll be paid less, but you can test out your routines and get comfortable in front of people before applying to private clubs. Clubs will often hire you as a substitute teacher first, then you can work your way up to regular staff. This gives the club a chance to see if you're good and if their clients like you. Think about teaching Kid Fitness or Teen Fitness programs as a way into bigger clubs with older clientele.

## Gardening/Landscaping

**Age:** 15/16
**Pay:** Anywhere from $8 to $13 an hour
**Dress Code:** Gardening grubs
**Job Prospects:** Good

**What to Expect:** Mowing and weeding lawns, spraying for pests, and pruning hedges. You could, for example, be part of a crew that moves around neighbourhoods doing garden maintenance. Or you could work for a school, park, cemetery, or golf course, whose grounds are so large that once you've completed the whole thing you have to start all over again because the place where you started has become overgrown.

**What's Expected of You:** Mow, weed, and prune. Just don't cut off any vital extremities with the hedge clippers.

**Required Knowledge Skills:** Lawn mower 101. Most of this stuff you can learn on the job, but some familiarity with gardening basics and equipment basics will help a lot.

**Where to Get Started:** This kind of job could be advertised at an employment centre or in the newspaper. To get a jump on those possibilities, start with your local Yellow Pages and try some gardening companies. The peak of garden care, of course, is in the summer, wherever you're living in Canada. You want to approach these companies in March or April, just before the rush hits, just when they're looking for more bodies to fill their summer crews. Look under Gardeners, but also Landscape Architects, Landscape Contractors & Designers, and Lawn Maintenance. There should be quite a few places to call, especially in a bigger city or suburb, with all those endless lawns. Large cemeteries need to hire people, as do schools, parks, and other large properties. Get creative. Try a Seniors Home or a neighbourhood of elderly people who may not be able to care for their gardens themselves.

## Provincial Parks and Resorts

**Age:** 16/17
**Pay:** From minimum to $10 an hour
**Dress Code:** Outdoor gear or professional leisure wear
**Job Prospects:** Fair
**What to Expect:** Provincial parks have plenty of summertime opportunities for students to be out of the city while earning their keep, e.g. picking up trash, overseeing campsites, and administration work. If you're physically fit and into hiking, there may be tours or camping trips that you could lead.

Resort jobs include cleaning and cooking staff, bar tending, maintenance, babysitting, and sports instructors. The problem is that many students apply for these jobs, since once you're hired you tend to live well around your work schedule, spending your days off in the sunshine, enjoying the fine and luxurious amenities that other poor sods have to pay for (that is, if they let the staff in the whirlpool). Apply early, and stand out. You may even want to try to visit the resort in person during the application process, even if it's a long haul from where you are.

**What's Expected of You:** That you do your best to show world-weary vacationers a good time so that they don't have to think much about anything. That you enjoy your job, but not so much that you're just lying around in the sun like a big dumb iguana.

**Required Knowledge Skills:** Experience or certification for the specific job you want.

**Where to Get Started:** For ideas and for phone numbers of some of the resorts and provincial parks in your area, a great place to start are the travel brochures handed out by each province.

Saskatchewan (305) 787-2300 or 1-800-667-7191
New Brunswick 1-800-561-0123
Newfoundland (709) 729-2830 or 1-800-563-6353
Alberta 1-800-661-8888
P.E.I. 1-800-463-4734
Ontario 1-800-668-2746
B.C. 1-800-663-6000
Quebec 1-800-363-7777
Nova Scotia 1-800-565-0000
Manitoba 1-800-665-0040
Northwest Territories 1-800-661-0788
Yukon (403) 667-5340

Also, check out a travel agency that specializes in getaways "up north," or wherever the hot spots for vacations are in your province. You want to get some selection of resorts or parks to choose from.

# WORKING WITH PHONES, FAXES, AND PHOTOCOPIERS

*"You have to learn to take orders and do what they want you to do. Always look busy."*

***—Misa (office)***

*"As a receptionist in a medical office I was dealing with scared, angry, and upset people for a good part of the time."*

***—Erin (reception)***

*"I spent the summer sitting in the same place looking at the same plant. But learning Word Perfect was interesting."*

***—Justine (reception)***

## General Office Clerk

**Age:** Usually 17 or 18, unless you have a connection (for instance, working in your parent's office)
**Pay:** Minimum wage to $10 an hour, depending on place and experience
**Dress Code:** Office attire: suits and skirts; can be more casual, depending on the office
**Job Prospects:** Good (especially with connections)
**What to Expect:** A summer student will be regarded as the perfect person to run off 63 copies of a two-sided, three-hole punched, 50-page memo. Data processing, typing, filing, faxing, photocopying, phoning, and taking calls and messages may be part of the job description.

This kind of work is a boon to organizers and detail people, since there's a certain satisfaction in being the reason the office runs so smoothly. If you return to the same office, you may find that your responsibilities increase—and you could find a way to make the jump to a more interesting full-time position after high school or university.
**What's Expected of You:** To be punctual, pleasant on the phone and in person, and organizationally and administratively splendid.

**Required Knowledge Skills:** As well as strong written and verbal skills, a familiarity with photocopiers and file cabinets. I'd also suggest a good working knowledge of at least one computer system. You need to be able to demonstrate that you know your way around computers at a data entry level and that they don't frighten you.

**Where to Get Started:** You could get a job in a publishing house, a food supplier's head office, a university, a film production office, an advertising agency, and so on to infinity. If you have absolutely no office connections, or if you're aiming for a particular office setting, you'll have to approach offices through cold calls.

Get hold of *The 1997 Canada Student Employment Guide* (the 1996 version will do), put out by the Student Employment Network. To order one you can call (416) 971-5090. The book is written, edited, and published by Kevin Makra, a total office job guru. It's meant for young people looking for full-time work after completing school, but it also mentions the availability of summer and part-time jobs for every listed company. Kevin lists phone numbers, contact names, and anything else you'll need to know to get started.

To spark your creativity and sense of possibility, I've come up with some interesting sounding offices. Remember, for each of these there are a million more, so don't use these as your only source.

Toronto International Film Festival
2 Carleton St., Toronto, ON M5B 1J3
(416) 967-7371

Mountain Equipment Co-op
1655 West 3rd Ave., Vancouver, BC V6J 1K1
(604) 732-1989 (head office)

Nestlé Simplot Foods
P.O. Box 70, Carberry, MB R0K 0H0
(204) 834-2136

Polygram Group Canada Inc.
1345 Denison St., Markham, ON L3R 5V2
(905) 415-9900

Information Systems Management Corporation
One Research Drive, Regina, SK S4S 7H1
(306) 781-5151

Intercon Security Ltd.
40 Sheppard Avenue West, 4th Fl., Willowdale, ON M2N 6K9
(416) 229-6811

## Receptionist

**Age:** 14 is the youngest, but 18 is the average starting age
**Pay:** Minimum to start, can increase to $10 an hour
**Dress Code:** Office attire
**Job Prospects:** Good
**What to Expect:** Receptionists are the front door to any company or business. They're the first voice you hear and the first face you see when you approach everything from a dental office to a brokers office. Therefore, expect to be the director of the action. You'll field, forward, and record calls. You'll be giving out information over and over ("We're located at Drake St. East, just north of Sawyer Avenue"). You'll also have periods of boredom when things slow down and nobody's calling or arriving for an appointment. (Bring a book.) You may also be expected to work on the computer and make coffee.
**What's Expected of You:** To be the patient, phone-literate "front person."
**Required Knowledge Skills:** You have to be polite, punctual, and good at writing down messages. There are reception jobs that require fluency in another language, so if you've got this it'll greatly increase your scope of possible jobs.
**Where to Get Started:** Use the ideas in the General Office entry to get you going. With all office jobs, contacts are the key. You may be able to get your initial experience in an office doing reception fill-in work for parents and friends of parents.

## File Clerk

**Age:** 15/16
**Pay:** Minimum wage to $9 an hour
**Dress Code:** Office attire
**Job Prospects:** Good
**What to Expect:** What else? Lots of files. It's not like being a filer is the most rockin' job in the world. I'm not going to kid you: you'll probably be bored. But on the

other hand you could get into the Zen of filing and spend your summer completely organizing the office and transcending your physical being. Who knows?
**What's Expected of You:** Organization, confidentiality, and a minimum of whining. If you want to take initiative (with permission of course) and update the files, I bet you'll be blessed as heaven-sent.
**Required Knowledge Skills:** The alphabet.
**Where to Get Started:** See the Office Clerk entry for ideas.

# Temping

**Age:** 14, but usually 17 or 18 as the unwritten minimum
**Pay:** Depending on your level of experience, anywhere from minimum wage to $12 an hour
**Dress Code:** Office attire
**Job Prospects:** Excellent, once you're with an agency
**What to Expect:** You're basically an office clerk, receptionist, word processor, or whatever the office needs you to be for as long as they need you. Also, note that the word temp is derived from the word temporary, as in not all the time. You'll have to be both patient and available, because you might not be called until the last minute for two days work after maybe a few weeks of not working.
**What's Expected of You:** Reliability is your number one asset to an agency. You're now representing the agency as well as the office you're working in. Doing a good job gets them repeat business and good word of mouth, so being on your best behaviour is more than something your mother would say, it's a temp's credo.
**Required Knowledge Skills:** The more office skills you have, the better chance the agency has of placing you. Start practising your speed typing.
**Where to Get Started:** Look in the phone book for agencies in your area. You'll need to approach them with your résumé and cover letter, and preferably with some office experience. You may want to approach them a few months before summer really hits and they fill up their extra hiring quota. The agency will interview you, and once you're accepted they, not the companies themselves, will offer you the jobs.

# WORKING WITH REGIONAL EVENTS

*"I saw all children—insane, nuts, badly behaved—pulling people off the slide. I did CPR and artificial resuscitation at least twice. There were picnicking families everywhere."*
**Shawn (waterslide lifeguard, Ontario Place)**

*"I spent the summer hauling crates and surrounded by women."*
**Dirk (CNE, restaurant)**

*"It was absolutely exhausting, there was so much to organize. But when it all came off it was amazing. And meeting the comics was cool."*
**Maureen (Montreal's Just for Laughs Festival)**

**What to Expect:** Every community and every regional centre has specific events and attractions that create jobs for students, particularly in the summer. Since these events are so different from city to city, county to county, province to province, I'll just give you some ideas about what these events might be, what kinds of things they might be looking for in summer help, and how to locate them.

First, there are specific tourist attractions that require mass hirings and that are usually filled by students. Here I'm thinking of theme parks, amusement parks, and exhibitions. The first ones that jump to my mind are Toronto's CNE (Canadian National Exhibition) and Vancouver's PNE (Pacific National Exhibition), Paramount Canada's Wonderland, and Montreal's La Ronde. These attractions are summer-oriented and require a ton of staff. Other attractions to consider are waterslide parks, malls like the West Edmonton mall (which incorporates a wave pool, train, and ice rink with shopping), Stanley Park's Aquarium in Vancouver, The Forks in Winnipeg, New Brunswick's Magnetic Hill Complex (a zoo, waterpark, and shops), and Ontario Place in Toronto.

Similar to these entertainment attractions are the events that mark a specific celebration in your area, like the Calgary Stampede and the Montreal Jazz Festival. These kinds of events require cleaners, ushers, gatekeepers, vendors, and endless upkeep jobs. They can also take place outside the summer months. Toronto's Royal Winter Fair, for example, is held every fall. For those of you who are into animals, this may be a great opportunity to get close to them.

Other options are concert venues and music events. The Winnipeg Folklorama and Folk Festival and other outdoor concert parks require a lot of help. During nighttime concerts or daytime sports events, stadiums require door people and program hawkers as well as cleaning staff and food sellers. Where do people in your area go to hear music, experience multicultural events, or see a baseball game? Answer that question and you may find other hiring possibilities.

In the larger cities, conventions are another option. If there's a convention of lawyers, dentists, labour union leaders, or guppie breeders heading your way, the hotels may be swamped and they'll need people to arrange all those "Hi my name is —" tags and point all the out-of-town partyers to the good restaurants.

**What's Expected of You:** The biggest thing that employers want to see during the hiring process is that you're knowledgeable about the event or attraction, that you're enthusiastic (because they want to know you can make all those out-of-towners so happy that they'll spend even more), and that you're willing to work hard for not a heck of a lot of money. For the most part you're looking at minimum wage, since they'll have to hire so many people. This is not to say that you can't move up the ladder and make more in subsequent summers, but just don't expect the big bucks now.

Re-read Chapter 6, particularly the part about mass hirings and some of the tricks and questions they tend to use in order to eliminate the undesirables. You'll get hired if you're prompt handing in your application, positive in your demeanour, and clear in your explanation of why you want to work at that particular event.

**Where to Get Started:** Contacting your provincial or local tourist board will hook you into the events that are happening in your geographical area for this year; you can also get phone numbers for some of the attractions. See "Resorts" for a list of the provincial numbers for tourist brochures to be sent to you, or to ask for their Internet sites if you want to surf for the information.

Since I don't know your community as intimately as you do, think about the activities that have been around since you were born but haven't attended since you were five. Nobody who lives in Toronto ever thinks of going up the CN Tower or visiting the Science Centre; they're so much a part of the city that we just don't think about it. Mentally approach your own city or town as if you were a tourist. What would you go see? You'll probably discover at least three job possibilities from your answer to that question. If you're still having trouble, head for your local library, get out that *Canadian Almanac and Directory,* and find the listings under "Events." You can even get the name of the event coordinators before you phone them.

# WORKING WITH SMALL PEOPLE (KIDS)

*"At overnight camp I was into it socially, but the money was crap."*
***—Jill (camp)***

*"Guarding is 40 percent lifeguard and 60 percent babysitter. Some guards never see any problems, but I had four rescues."*
***—Thecla (lifeguarding)***

*"Lifeguarding paid for my Ph.D. . . . you get paid to talk to people."*
***—Chris (lifeguarding)***

## Camp Jobs

**Age:** counsellors in training (CITs) 15/16; counsellors 16 and up
**Pay:** From room and board to $2,000 for Programming Heads
**Dress Code:** Grubs
**Job Prospects:** Excellent
**What to Expect:** Camp jobs have always been popular among students, because they're a fun way to spend a summer partying it up in a beautiful, leisurely setting. Don't be fooled, though; their "non-serious" reputation can lure many people into thinking that it's all easy work, when in fact it's a 24-hour-a-day job.

Summer camps are usually in business from the beginning of July to the end of August, with a pre-camp session the last week in June during which the counsellors prepare for the coming summer sessions. So if you're a university student, it's possible to have another job before camp starts. Tree-planting season, for instance, is mostly May and June and so will give you the chance to make some money beforehand. And having solved your money woes, you can simply enjoy the summer camp experience.

There are two or three kinds of jobs at summer camp, and you should consider which you'd prefer. There's the standard counsellor job, for a group of kids ranging from six or seven to fifteen or sixteen. You'll be responsible for their well-being 24 hours a day. If you have skills in a particular area you can either find a camp where you can work on just that program, or where you can be a counsellor as well.

The other option is to work for a day camp, which usually runs only five days a week and functions as a replacement for school activities during the summer. Day camp counsellors usually make better money, but because you're in the city with more time off you tend to spend more, whereas at overnight camp your costs are limited to your days off.

**What's Expected of You:** A camp counsellor at an overnight camp is a 24-hour-a-day job. Although the social life is fantastic (and you'll get no sleep trying to enjoy it), you're also responsible for the safety, well-being, and entertainment of children whose parents have paid good money to see a popsicle stick birdcage and a swimming badge by the end of the summer. Leadership, enthusiasm, and a way with kids (or at least a general liking for the little creatures) are all good qualities to have and to emphasize when applying.

**Required Knowledge Skills:** Any camp around a lake will require some form of swimming competency, and probably a specific swimming badge, usually Bronze Cross Level.

If you have any skills like sailing, windsurfing, water-skiing, swimming, archery, riflery, arts and crafts, trampoline, drama, canoeing, snorkling, tennis, basketball, or fencing, your employability increases immensely. Even if you've attended camp and learned as a camper, this is often enough to qualify for an entry-level camp position.

**Where to Get Started:** Most of the following organizations have publications that list member camps and their specifics (i.e., size, length of sessions, activities, phone numbers). Some of these places may also have a service where in January you can fill out a general job application that will be made available for camp directors. I still recommend that you go directly to the source and contact each camp individually.

Canadian Camping Association/Association des camps du Canada
1810 Avenue Road, Ste. 303, Toronto, ON M5M 3Z2
(416) 781-4717

Alberta Camping Association (ACA)
Percy Page Centre, 11759 Groat Rd., Edmonton, AB T5M 3K6
(403) 453-8570

Association de Camps du Quebec
4545 Ave Pierre de Coubertin, P.O. Box 1000
Station M, Montreal, PQ H1V 3R2
(514) 252-3113 or (only in Quebec) 1-800-361-3586
(Or, send a cheque for $3.19 and ask for their all-inclusive booklet that lists 116 camps in Quebec.)

British Columbia Camping Association
3302 Senkler Rd., Belcarra, BC B3H 4S3
Send $2 with stamped, self-addressed envelope.

Camping Association of Nova Scotia
P.O. Box 3243, South Halifax, NS B3J 3H5
(902) 865-3523

Manitoba Camping Association
194A Sherbrook St., Winnipeg, MB R3C 2B6
(204) 784-1134

New Brunswick Camping Association
105-440 Wilsey Rd., Fredericton, NB E3B 7G5
(506) 459-1929

Newfoundland & Labrador Camping Association
c/o Circle Square Ranch, Box 1120,
Manual, NF A1W 1N6
(709) 781-0183

Ontario Camping Association (OCA)
2-1806 Avenue Road, Toronto, ON M5M 3Z1
(416) 781-0525

Saskatchewan Camping Association
c/o Saskatoon YMCA, 25-22 St. East, Saskatoon, SK S7K 0C7
(306) 652-7515

# Lifeguarding

**Age:** With an NLS you may lifeguard with others at 16; at 17 you can lifeguard on your own
**Pay:** *Municipal:* $8 an hour and up. *Pool Companies:* just above minimum; rises with added skills (for instance, 30¢ an hour more for having First Aid). *Camps:* Least profitable (see Camps entry).
**Dress Code:** Bathing suit and probably a light, comfortable uniform
**Job Prospects:** Good
**What to Expect:** Who could deny the excitement of *Baywatch?* But your lifesaving skills mean nothing to the kids who run on the deck or to the concerned parents who demand to know why little Johnny isn't in the Olympics, much less why he's not getting his Red swimming badge.

*Municipal City Pools:* Apply early. The work is done with a team of guards in rotating shifts, with a 15-minute break (usually to get out of the sun) every hour. The average lifeguard can expect to get about 35 to 40 hours of work a week.

There's no slacking allowed, though. You're responsible not only for your swimmers but for your performance as a guard. There are regular evaluations, surprise drills, and on-site superiors. Each guard is also expected to do weekly fitness, either in the pool or elsewhere. Don't even expect to be idle when it rains, since that's the perfect time for pool cleaning and maintenance.

*Small Pools:* Getting a job with companies that are responsible for running apartment pools is relatively easy, since they usually manage a lot of pools. Because apartment pools are small, they're a one-person job. You'll end up knowing a lot more about pool maintenance as well as guarding. Since you're the only guard you'll probably have only one or two breaks during the day, but you do get a half or a full hour for lunch and dinner. The pools are usually small and hence easy to guard, but you do tend to do more babysitting. If you're hired by a pool company you will, for the most part, be your own boss. A supervisor may check in on you once or twice a week but the responsibility is yours. That can mean using your own discretion as to when to close the pool, among other things. The pay is about $7 an hour for a first-timer, depending on your badges and courses.

Another angle on the smaller pools is to get a job with the YMCA or similar club facilities. Again you're most often left in charge. Many holiday resorts that offer summer getaways have pools that need tending, and they may even have programmed water activities. (See Resort section.)

*Camp Guarding:* If the resort idea isn't panning out and kids are more your forte, there's always space on camp rosters for good lifeguards and swim teachers.

**Required Knowledge Skills:** Once you have the necessary lifeguarding requirements, getting an initial pool job is fairly easy. The Red Cross Bronze Medallion and Bronze Cross badges are the main requirements, but the National Lifeguard badge, a certified First Aid course, and a CPR course will help you get the guard job and increase your pay. If you wish to teach swimming as well as lifeguarding, you'll also need a Leaders badge.

*First Aid and CPR:* St. John's Ambulance offers a course in Standard First Aid, plus a basic rescuer CPR that's usually a three-day program and costs about $120. That may seem like a lot of cash, but if you're planning to work in this field it's an invaluable investment. In order to find the regional St. John's Ambulance closest to you, contact:

St. John's Ambulance (Head Office)
312 Laurier Ave. East, Ottawa, ON K1N 6P6
(613) 236-7461

You could also try your local recreation centre/YMCA for courses. Some high schools offer First Aid in their gym credit, or as an extra-curricular activity. The key is to get a certificate that says you're proficient in First Aid procedures.

Also handy for working at a pool is some pool maintenance. Even if you only know how to jump-start a filter system or test the water's chlorination levels you could be paid a bit more.

**Where to Get Started:** Contact your local municipal board to find out where the pools in your area are and whether there's a central hiring process. For private pool guarding, find out who runs the pools in your area. You could ask the superintendent at an apartment or housing complex (with a pool that advertises a lifeguard) what company provides them with the service. Also, look in the Yellow Pages under Swimming Pools or Property Management companies. For camps, you'll have to apply to each one separately.

YMCA Head Office
(416) 928-9622
(ask for the one nearest you)

## Babysitter

**Age:** 12 and up (should be 14 for very young children)
**Pay:** $3.50 to $7 an hour (depending on age and experience), or a lump sum for the evening
**Dress Code:** Presentable, comfortable clothes
**Job Prospects:** Excellent
**What to Expect:** Sometimes you'll get children who cry the entire time their parents are gone, sometimes you'll get children who are terrors and refuse to obey you, and sometimes you'll babysit dream children who worship you and just want to play hide'n'go seek for hours on end.

Expectations can differ from parent to parent. It's important to clarify these up front so that you know your limitations. You want to know the names and ages of the kids, the parents' expectations of what they want you to do, if any of the kids have medical problems, when you'll start and finish, any household routines, your transportation to and from the home, numbers where the parents can be reached, and whether you can eat there.

Don't be afraid to say no to a situation if you feel you can't handle it, or if there's something about it you don't like. Your comfort level should come first so that you can do your job well. That includes saying no to a drunk dad who offers you a ride home after coming back from a party (true story). Make sure that you've got a way home arranged independent of your employers, unless you well and truly trust them to see you home safely.

**What's Expected of You:** The best babysitters are punctual, responsible, honest, and like children. You're functioning in place of a parent, and—although it's easy to forget when Susie's asleep upstairs, you're chowing down on cold pizza, and your favourite sitcom's on—if anything goes wrong it's you and you alone in charge. Being sensitive to the needs of children—their fears about their parents being away, or the dark, or the drink of water they need before going to sleep—is what this job is about. Ask the questions that will tune you into each particular household. Clean up after yourself and never, ever leave the children alone for any reason.
**Required Knowledge Skills:** First Aid is a very good skill to have. Also handy, although not absolutely essential, are babysitting courses, which will provide you with a certificate. St. John's Ambulance offers a course called "What Every

Babysitter Should Know" for about $35, which includes a book and a certificate. Also offered are child and infant CPR, and children's First Aid.

A book you can read for a start is called *The Babysitters Handbook* by Carol Greene. It's published by Random House, in association with St. John's Ambulance.

**Where to Get Started:** If you're on the young end of the age scale and you want to get into babysitting, you may want to provide trial runs for parents, or offer to help out family members while they go shopping in order to gain some experience that you can then parlay into paid work. Often babysitting jobs come up through friends of your parents or neighbours with children. If you're surrounded by childless people, you could look into advertising locally. Put an ad up in your local supermarket or library. In your ad or poster, refer to your First Aid skills and note that references will be provided.

## Nanny

**Age:** 18 and up (agencies)
**Pay:** $5 to $8.50 an hour
**Dress Code:** Presentable, comfortable clothes
**Job Prospects:** Fair
**What to Expect:** Whether you're a live-in or a nanny with specific regular hours, you can expect to be—you got it—taking care of kids for most of the day. A nanny is essentially a babysitter with slightly higher pay and a consistent day in, day out job. You're going to be spending more than TV-watching time with your charges, so be prepared to play games, do crafts, make lunch, and go for walks to the park. Also expect to see the best and worst of your charges. Since you see them every day, you'll cease to be the "special" babysitter and instead become part of the regular household routine.

There's also the possibility that a family could hire you to go on their vacation with them. This "vacation" is still a job for you, but you can do your glorified babysitting in the luxurious setting of a cottage or resort.

**What's Expected of You:** As in all kid jobs, you're going to be responsible for the health and safety of someone else's child. Agencies require you to be eighteen so that they can better guarantee the job you'll do.

**Required Knowledge Skills:** First Aid is a must. Also, CPR and CPR for infants is a good idea. (See Lifeguarding and Babysitting entries.) An agency will definitely require references, and any parent worth their salt will also require references if they're hiring on their own.

**Where to Get Started:** Look in the classified ads under Domestic Help, or apply to an agency. The benefit of an agency is that if they accept you you'll get placed with a family. However, they aren't essential in this field.

## Tutor

**Age:** 15 or 16 is average

**Pay:** Under $8 when starting out, but up to $10 an hour with more experience

**Dress Code:** Presentable, not quite office wear

**Job Prospects:** Good

**What to Expect:** If you're good with kids and good with schoolwork, this job is tailor-made.

**What's Expected of You:** To be patient, caring, and organized. Don't take on a subject you're not familiar with, unless you're prepared to do your own review of it. Thinking of creative ways to help students approach the material may also be in order. Remember that you're being hired to supplement class time.

**Required Knowledge Skills:** You'll have to know well the subject you're tutoring.

**Where to Get Started:** The Guidance Department in your high school, or former high school, is a good place to start. They and your teachers could give you needed references as well. You could also advertise locally, or try connections. For younger children, try talking to primary and elementary school teachers to find out if they know of any parents looking for help.

# WORKING WITH TECHIES

*"With computers I recommend that you should go further and learn more. Once you're over your computer phobia they're easy to use. The more computer experience you have, the better off you are."*
***—Ellen (mainframe programmer)***

*"If you know your stuff you can ask for the big bucks."*
***—Al (Web site designer)***

*"The computer industry is aware that young people know the new tricks."*
***—Tiffany (Web site manager/producer)***

## Word/Data Processer

**Age:** 14/15
**Pay:** $8 to $16 an hour
**Dress Code:** Office wear if in the corporate world, more casual depending on the office situation
**Job Prospects:** Excellent
**What to Expect:** Some organization of the material, but accurate inputting is the bottom-line expectation. You may be entering bar codes of material that the office has received, you may be typing up letters and memos, or you may be entering names and phone numbers into a newly created data base.

The scope of the job gets extended if your employer allows you to create the data entry program. If you were able, for instance, to create a program for a real estate office that catalogued all their clients, houses, and prices, all of which could be called up using key words, that would be a pretty amazing summer project. However, with any new data base someone has to enter all the information that's previously been in files or random desk drawers. And guess what—that person is probably going to be you. Organizers unite!
**What's Expected of You:** Accurate entries. Working knowledge of the computer program.

**Required Knowledge Skills:** Become proficient in more than one or two word processing programs. If you understand Microsoft Word, Windows '95, and Word Perfect, you'll be equipped to understand most office computers.
**Where to Get Started:** Like an office clerk, the employment opportunities are endless. You just have to hook up with an office or similar situation that has a computer system and data waiting to be entered. This can be anything from legal offices to warehouses. Get creative and use your connections. Re-read the Office Clerk entry for ideas.

# Technical Support

**Age:** 16 (though you'll really have to demonstrate that you can communicate your knowledge to others)
**Pay:** $10 to $20 an hour
**Dress Code:** None—techies tend to look like they've never heard of a dress code
**Job Prospects:** Excellent (if you know your stuff)
**What to Expect:** Lots of questions. Lots and lots of questions. Lots and lots of dumb questions. For instance, you'll be working with someone who can't get their computer to boot. You'll get them to push all the different buttons. Then you'll ask them if it's plugged in and they'll say no.

In order to do this job you'll have to have a good understanding of several different computer models, the Internet, and how to communicate your knowledge to others. You could be working for an Internet service provider, where you help someone configure their computer to start cruising the Net. Or you could be a service support person who helps a customer figure out why, for instance, they've got a memory problem. If you've got the knowledge and expertise you can work freelance and offer yourself as either a teacher or someone who'll configure other people's computers and computer systems.
**What's Expected of You:** You can't just be boy/girl genius computer whiz. Technical support requires that you "support" the user in solving their own problems. You'll often be doing this over the phone, and you'll have to be able to communicate with a beginner who doesn't know the language. One support staff member told the story of a woman who kept saying that her coffee cup holder wouldn't work. When questioned, she reiterated that the coffee cup holder that

came with her computer didn't slide out any more. It turns out that she was talking about her CD-ROM drive. This story sums up both the simplicity and complexity of the job.

**Required Knowledge Skills:** An intimate knowledge of whatever aspect of computers you wish to provide help for. An ability to impart that knowledge to someone who has no clue what you're talking about.

**Where to Get Started:** Since Internet service providers need a ton of people, you can start there. Call providers in your area and ask for Call Support or the Help Desk to get you in the right area. You can also look to striking out on your own, using connections to offer your services to either companies or individual users.

# Web Sites (programming, upkeep, and designers)

**Age:** 16

**Pay:** $10 an hour (easy stuff) to $15 to $20 an hour (interactive programming)

**Dress Code:** Slim to none—no suits necessary

**Job Prospects:** Good to Excellent (if you know your stuff)

**What to Expect:** There's a nice mix of technology and creativity in jobs around Web site operations. Once you've mastered the technology and the programming you'll be able to create Web pages that are fun, interesting, and stimulating.

The first level of work involves using HTML (Hyper Text Markup Language), a really simple programming lingo that allows you to easily edit Web pages. There are jobs that require you to use this programming to lay out new material on the Web page, edit it, and link it to other pages. You may also be responsible for the upkeep of the page, keeping information current, and monitoring responses.

As you learn more programming your involvement with the pages can become more complex. The really interesting pages are interactive, have images that move, and are engaging to the user. Once you learn the harder programming (C+, C++, Perl, Java) that does the action, and more of the database-type programming (CGI, Dbase) that contains the information, you'll become very valuable to any kind of multimedia company.

As quoted above, computer companies understand that young people know the new tricks. There are a ton of small and large companies to choose from and this is a very entrepreneurial business.

**Required Knowledge Skills:** Definitely HTML to start. Even if you just picked up a book you'd probably grasp most of it over a weekend. A working understanding of the Internet and Netscape. To advance, pick up C+ and C++, Perl, and Java. Java is the hot new program that the schools and companies seem to be embracing. The way to get ahead is to advance to more hardcore, interactive, and hence more useful programming. Anything to do with databases that you can throw in would help you better manipulate the programs and grab salient data for use on the page.

**Where to Get Started:** Small companies with smaller budgets consider students a godsend. One employer recommended to me that students send e-mails to the companies that create sites they like. You can also fax your résumé or go by word of mouth.

If you get into Web site creation your name will become known in computer circles. You may get more work as a result of people liking the work you've already done. The programming community is still pretty small, so there's plenty of room to make your mark.

## Image Makers and Digital Artists

**Age:** 18/19 for company interns, may be younger in other situations
**Pay:** $15 an hour and up
**Dress Code:** None, in fact dress down to be taken seriously
**Job Prospects:** Good (if you're skilled)
**What to Expect:** Calling all artists! Not making any money in oil paints? Can't get a gallery to show your work? Consider being a digital artist and getting both exposure and pay for doing what you love.

Imaging, and the more complex digital artistry, are growing fields for future jobs. Imaging is another aspect of the Web site editing discussed above. It involves online editing and manipulating the pictures that go with the edited text. For instance, think of a weekly magazine that puts its stories online. You may be in charge of recreating the material for the computer—laying it out, editing, and fitting the pictures with the text.

As your knowledge grows so does the complexity. Your work will become more varied as you learn to scan and manipulate an image, and change or add elements. You could do everything from 3D images for slot machines to creating digital presentations for multimedia companies. Being able to adapt your creativity to computer technology will really take you far. One computer guy I talked to told me that everyone good at art in his high school is now doing some form of digital art. You could be creating CD covers, 3D art, or even taking the digital creativity further, for use, say, in films like *Toy Story*. This area is a new frontier for job creation, so the only limits to how you can apply your knowledge are set by you.

**What's Expected of You:** This is art for a business purpose, so whatever your creative process, when the customers want it, they want it now. Also needed: a huge amount of creativity. This is an industry that wants you to stretch.

**Required Knowledge Skills:** Programs for artistry. The basic ones include Dolby Photo Shop, Corel Draw, and Freehand and Illustrator. The programs that do layout include Pagemaker and Quark Xpress. You'll need to get a handle on at least Dolby Photo Shop and Quark to get started.

**Where to Get Started:** Again, this will take some research on your part. You'll need to find a company or niche that matches your artistic interests. You could start out doing the imaging layout for Web pages, but remember that once you get into the digital design world your work can speak for you. Keep practising with the programs, and apply through e-mails, faxes, and cold calls to the various companies that suit your artistic taste.

# WORKING WITH THINGS (PAINTBRUSHES, POWER TOOLS, DUSTRAGS, AND DIRTBIKES)

*"There was nothing good about the job. I made a lot of money because I never went out, and since I worked the night shift I never ate, so I lost twenty pounds. It made me want to go to back to school."*

***—Adam (assembly line)***

*"The rule of thumb is one serious accident a year."*

***—Manju (bike courier)***

*"It's not the crashing I mind, it's getting run over afterwards."*
***—Kasper (bike courier)***

*"By the end of the summer you never wanted to clean another toilet again."*
***—Dilip (cottage cleaning)***

*"It's great seeing a project from start to finish. Still, with a fifty-hour work week it gets tiring, fast."*
***—Chris M. (construction)***

# Painting

**Age:** 15/16 youngest, but usually university students
**Pay:** Most of the time it's piece work, so it could be less than minimum wage or $12, depending on your speed of work
**Dress Code:** Coveralls and anything that can be safely paint-splattered
**Job Prospects:** Good
**What to Expect:** Painting a house isn't like painting a picture. Although being neat and staying in the lines is important, the bottom line is that painting is hard manual labour. Not only do you have to keep those arm strokes going all day, but you'll be lugging around ladders, paint cans, and other equipment. Further, you can't be afraid of heights, because you'll end up dangling from strange places trying to get that last, hard-to-reach corner.

Be prepared to get covered in paint. Paint will be your life. It'll be the smell you smell when you start the day and it'll coat your hands when you end it. Customers will talk to you about paint, you'll consider painting strategies, and when you go to bed at night you'll probably dream of paint. By the same token, you'll be outside (unless you're doing indoor painting, of course) in the sunshine, doing a task with a tangible result. The other bonus is that you'll have picked up a trade that'll be useful to you the rest of your life, especially when it comes to painting your own house or apartment.
**What's Expected of You:** Hard work. The most quality done in the least amount of time.
**Required Knowledge Skills:** Most companies will train you on site.

**Where to Get Started:** Obviously, you'll need to approach painting companies and offer your services. The advantage is that with our Canadian weather, there's a definite outdoor paint season for which employers have to hire lots of people. Your best bet is to approach these companies in March about the possibility of working for them. Find out when their heavy season starts. If a lack of experience is holding you back, offer to paint for someone on a volunteer basis, for example at home or for a church or charity.

# Warehouse/Shipping

**Age:** 16
**Pay:** $9 to $14 an hour, with overtime at night
**Dress Code:** Overalls, work wear, or regulation clothing
**Job Prospects:** Good
**What to Expect:** Like most of these jobs, shipping and warehouse work is hard physical labour that will require your concentration to complete safely. Imagine a 40,000 ton container that can hold four moving trucks and is filled to the brim with boxes containing more boxes of frozen fishless cod balls. Your job: unload. That's shipping in a nutshell. It's heavy, constant work that you could do for twelve hours at a stretch.

At some point you'll likely be trained to use a forklift (which, I'm told, is incredibly fun to operate). The forklift seems to make this job universally more interesting than just lifting, but no one claimed that this particular summer employment was a mind-blower. Dull, repetitive, but lots of money.

You may also find that you're involved in the administrative aspect of shipping, which includes inventory, filing, and retrieving and cataloguing materials.
**What's Expected of You:** Consistent hard labour.
**Required Knowledge Skills:** None.
**Where to Get Started:** A contact may get you started, but it's been recommended to me that if you get in touch with different warehouses and ask around, jobs should be available. You want to find out if there's a time when they'll be moving a lot of product, and so will be more likely to need extra help. Although many warehouses are unionized they may still need extra labourers, so make yourself useful.

# Assembly Line/Factory Work

**Age:** 16
**Pay:** $8 to $11 an hour, 8-hour shifts, with extra for overtime
**Dress Code:** No loose clothing
**Job Prospects:** Good
**What to Expect:** The same thing over and over again. The same thing over and over again. The same thing over and over again. The same thing over and over again. You think this sentence is dull after four readings? Try doing the same thing hundreds of times and see how you feel about it. You can expect to do the same motion, perform the same action, again and again. For instance, one student had an assembly line job that consisted solely of sticking plastic cards to a piece of paper. He had a well of glue and a stack of cards and he had to stick a card to every piece of paper that came his way. That was his summer.

In factory work you may not being doing something specific, as you would on an assembly line, but you may be the pair of eyes that checks the product in its last stages. You have to be on the look-out and really check what's going through the machines, because if you miss a problem in things like food or computer chips there could be severe consequences. You're required to be present and focused, even though you've seen the same thing for the last seven hours.

You may also find yourself at a machine, responsible for drilling a precise hole in a precise place on a piece of metal. Again, you'll have to stay focused, not only to keep the work consistent but for your own safety. There are several types of machinery you may end up using.

These are good jobs that pay you well for the difficulty of being consistent and precise in the face of overwhelming boredom. There's also a possibility of becoming a supervisor or manager of your particular section. This is not a job that's going to expand your mind or challenge your perceptions of the universe. The hard part of the job is being able to stand the repetitiveness. Don't do this job if you have a wandering mind or a huge rebellious streak. You may do more damage than simply losing your job.
**What's Expected of You:** The same job, over and over again. No goofing off.
**Required Knowledge Skills:** None, because you'll know your particular job inside out by Day Two.

**Where to Get Started:** Whether it's through a contact, a friend who works at a factory, or through a newspaper or job board ad, you'll need to be in a vicinity that has factory and assembly plants. That may seem rather obvious, but a huge computer plant is not likely to be sitting at the end of your block. You'll have to source out the possibilities in your area for this type of work.

# Construction

**Age:** 19 (unless it's a private contractor)
**Pay:** $8 to $12 an hour
**Dress Code:** Hard work wear
**Job Prospects:** Fair
**What to Expect:** Although I've met and talked to students who've done construction jobs, what we conceive of as construction (dusty sites, men in yellow hats, big drills) is probably not a job area that hires a lot of students. Construction jobs are more likely going to come to you in the form of private contractors, including your parents, who are into re-finishing their home or cottage and need willing labour. And perhaps even cheap labour. From these kinds of jobs you can learn the basics of laying and finishing floors, fibreglass installation, roofing, or whatever else the particular job entails. You won't be involved in design or complex installations for the most part, but you can see a product through from start to finish and have a hand in constructing it. It may be better to think of these jobs more as "handyman/woman" jobs than out-and-out construction. That being said, I'm sure some of you will figure out a way onto a huge construction site.
**What's Expected of You:** Hard physical labour, and a quality job (so that the house doesn't fall down two days after you're finished).
**Required Knowledge Skills:** You'll probably pick up all sorts of skills in carpentry, drilling, and using all kinds of power tools.
**Where to Get Started:** This is a job you'll have to be pro-active to find. Go to the employment centres and look on the job boards, and talk to friends who might be doing similar work or who've worked for a specific company in the past. One student I talked to got his construction job by calling every construction company in the phone book until he hit a foreman who'd just fired somebody and needed a replacement that minute. Another way to find companies is to check out neighbourhoods where construction is underway and determine the company from the name on the sign or on the truck outside.

# Maintenance

**Age:** 16
**Pay:** $8 to $15 per hour, depending on how much you're responsible for
**Dress Code:** Coveralls
**Job Prospects:** Fair
**What to Expect:** Maintenance work comes in varied forms, and you could be working on your own or as someone's assistant. Most maintenance jobs involve working for a particular building. You could be changing lightbulbs, painting and caulking, sweeping and mopping, fixing door handles, and making sure the inside of the building looks good. You may also be responsible for the outside of the building—shovelling, raking, or planting flowers and lawn mowing, depending on the season. Although you can expect to deal with all kinds of little problems, for the true maintenance emergencies you'll probably have the authority to call the plumber or electrician. If you're someone's assistant, expect to be doing the lowest order of work—cleaning up pigeon poop or holding the ladder. But you'll most likely learn more and use more tools.
**What's Expected of You:** This is work that needs to be completed, but it can move at its own pace. You'll have to be responsible for getting the work done, particularly if there's no one checking up on you regularly.
**Required Knowledge Skills:** Having some ability to find your way around a toolbox. If you don't know the difference between a wrench and a pair of pliers, this job probably isn't for you. The more familiar you are with basic handy work, the more valuable an employee you'll be.
**Where to Get Started:** This is the kind of job that may be advertised in the papers or on job boards. You could also try contacts who own or manage different buildings and who might need an assistant. Summer is the time when owners like to make repairs and do extra work, which is why it'd be a good time to approach building managers in your neighbourhood. Another excellent source of work are schools. They often do their repair or maintenance work during the summer, or they may just need someone to look after the place for a couple of months. For that you may need to approach the local school board as well as the schools, and start a couple of months early. Any building needs regular maintenance, so look out your window and you'll see plenty of opportunity.

If you're quite skilled at a lot of different maintenance jobs you could also advertise yourself as a handyperson who could be hired by the day or hour. Many homes have two or three tasks that never get done, and you could offer to be the person who builds the composter, hangs the old mirror from the attic, fixes the leaky faucet, and cleans the garage.

## Bike/Walking Courier

MAR

**Age:** 17/18
**Pay:** Varies from city to city; usually piece work. It could be $50 or $80 a day depending on your experience, number of drops, and speed.
**Dress Code:** Biker shorts chic, plus radio
**Job Prospects:** Good, especially in the winter when they're desperate for riders
**What to Expect:** Okay, I'm going to say this and then you can make up your own mind. Bike couriering is a dangerous job. If you bike carefully, you'll make no money (see above quote re one serious accident a year). Catch my drift? This job is for people who are truly gonzo and use "extreme" to describe a tame weekend.

Bike couriers weave in and out of city traffic, discover back routes and alley ways, and do whatever they have to to make a drop to make the money to get the next assignment. As a beginner, you'll have the added drawback of not knowing the dispatcher. The dispatcher is the one who sets up the good drops versus the cross-town marathons, and so you want to be on that person's good side a.s.a.p.

The bigger the city and the tighter the downtown core, the easier it is to make good money, even though the danger factor is ever-present. Some cities have walking couriers who take the subway or (obviously) walk to make deliveries.
**What's Expected of You:** You'll make the delivery as soon as possible. No questions asked as to how you managed. Incredible physical fitness, fast.
**Required Knowledge Skills:** How to avoid people who open their car doors without looking. How to be both a car and a pedestrian, depending on whose right of way it is. You have to be a little bit crazy.
**Where to Get Started:** Given the tough conditions of the job, most bike courier companies are always looking for new recruits. Probably the hardest time to get a job is right at the beginning of summer, particularly if university students getting out of school get there first. Check back later though, because I guarantee that some of them will drop out before too long.

# House Cleaning

**Age:** 16
**Pay:** $70 to $100 per house (depending on size and how much you work); could be around $10 to $14 an hour
**Dress Code:** Comfortable cleaning clothes
**Job Prospects:** *Agency*: Good Luck; *On your own or with contacts*: Good
**What to Expect:** You know how your mother keeps asking you to clean your room? Imagine her surprise if you told her you were spending the summer cleaning other people's rooms. Now I don't think you have to be a neat freak in order to do this job, but you do have to enjoy cleaning. You'll be dusting, cleaning toilets, mopping, cleaning out the fridge, vacuuming, polishing, and tidying. You'll be setting your own hours and working at your own pace, which means that you could make the same money in three hours or six hours, depending on your speed.

If you're working at one house regularly you'll have to create a cleaning plan. If you work there once a week, you can do all the general chores and then rotate big projects like the fridge or the basement or the windows. If you're there only once a month, you'll have to do everything possible. The best way to do consistent work is to go one room at a time and make sure each is completed to your satisfaction before moving on.

If you're doing this on your own you'll need to set out expectations with each employer. The phrase "I don't do windows" is well known in popular culture, but you'll have to decide if you do indeed do windows, or laundry, or any of the other things that employers might try to include. Ask the employer to supply the cleaning products, and make a list of what you'll need. Find out which are the most important jobs so that you can be sure to complete them every time you work.

Expect that some people will tidy up for you, and that some people will figure that since you're coming, why bother even trying to clean? The bottom line is that on some level you have to enjoy cleaning; the rhythm of scrubbing the tub or the satisfaction of seeing a room look better once you've finished it. If you don't find pleasure in cleaning, this job is going to sour really quickly.
**What's Expected of You:** That you clean efficiently and that the employer can see the difference in you being there. You'll also be expected to be honest and trustworthy; remember that people are letting you into their homes. Don't get too personal with your employers, since you're there to do a job for them. Be organized. Part of cleaning is having a routine.

**Required Knowledge Skills:** Knowing the cleaning products that work for you. Familiarity with vacuum dustbags. Getting off those rubber gloves when your hands are all sweaty.

**Where to Get Started:** During the time this book was researched (by superstar Nicole), we encountered much suspicion and plain bad vibes from the cleaning companies we tried to talk to. This could just be our experience and there may well be many nice, wonderful agencies that would love to have you working for them. But if you encounter the same displeasure we did, we recommend going out on your own. That's how all the students we talked to managed anyway. One student did the homes of her mother's friends. One student joined a company of students that worked in an area with a lot of summer homes and cottages. Another became an entrepreneur, asking people through door-to-door visits and getting customers to recommend her to others. She eventually built up a solid customer base that even worked around her school schedule. Some students worked with a partner, and some worked alone. There's a lot of room for your own creativity in getting this kind of work, and in the end it's probably better not to depend on an agency that will take a cut and regulate your progress. The advantage of an agency is that they provide the jobs. But if you have a lot of initiative, the agency really isn't necessary.

# PART 3

# ALTERNATIVES THAT YOUR PARENTS MIGHT NOT HAVE MENTIONED

# Options that Don't Pay Cash

No cash! No cash! What are you doing to me Karen? I bought this stupid book to get a dumb job so that I could make money, and now you want to tell me I could spend my summer fritting away my time doing something that would pay me *no cash*. Thanks a lot.

Okay, are you done? I know, I know, you bought the book under the strange pretense that you'd be looking for work this summer, you'd be getting a pay cheque, and you, your parents, your love interest, the dog . . . everyone would be happy. But some of you may not have considered other options that could be fruitful not only this summer, but later down the road. Please stop throwing things and I'll explain.

You have some choices (because whether you know it or not, you always have choices. It just depends on how committed you are to making them happen) that aren't as straightfoward as: Get a résumé, Get a job, Get a pay cheque. I agree that that's a pretty decent scenario, and one that I've been encouraging for about two hundred pages, but now I want to open the window for you a little more. There are certain other things you can do, for the whole summer or in conjunction with a job, that may get you even further than a job alone could.

What if you took a course that got you ahead in school? What if you took a course that had nothing to do with school but was something you were really interested in? What if you took that course in another city or country? Or what if you ditched the course and saw the world? What if you saw the world in a whole new way because you took a trip that challenged every idea or notion you ever had? Or what if you didn't get a job, and instead offered your services *for free* to someone? And, finally, what if you came up with an idea for your own job and you got money and put it into motion and had your own business?

Now I want to say something up front, just so we're all clear. I, through various circumstances both good and bad, was in the fortunate position to experience many of the things that I'll be outlining here. I was privileged, no question about it (I know this particularly well, because I've spent this year in relative working-at-a-video-store poverty). Reading this book are many different people in different situations. Some of you can get the money from your parents. Some of you will have to persuade your parents that the money they'll give you will be worth it. And there are some of you whose parents just don't have the money, whether they think you've got a good idea or not. You're not going to be racing off to Europe any time soon, and you don't have the time to be volunteering your life away.

But don't get hooked on the story that you can't do anything because you have no money. You can—you just have to work harder. If you want to get ahead by volunteering, do it around your schedule. If you wait tables at night, give up two hours of sleep to volunteer at that radio station during the day. The biggest barrier is the one in your head that says it's impossible. As soon as you get over that, you'll start looking for ways to make it happen.

For those of you who feel that all you need in order to do some of these things is a miraculous transformation in the way your parents see you, I've got that covered too. I'm going to talk a little bit about the ways you can make this stuff happen, even if your parents and guardians would never ever in a million years think that doing things for no money is a good idea.

An up-front hint: take responsibility for what you want to do and make what needs to happen happen. We'll talk. For now, let me tantalize you with some alternatives to summer employment. . . .

## Summer Courses

Going to summer school is not the exact same thing as regular school, and that has its advantages. First, summer can't help but be a mellower time. Students chill, teachers chill, and it's really too hot to get excited about anything. A kind of laid-back ease and solidarity begins to form in summer classes, and that can be conducive to actually learning something—and maybe even enjoying it. If that's too much to handle, think of it this way: since that calculus class will be the only one you have to think about you'll have a great shot at doing well in it, as opposed to during the school year when you're going to blow it off for other classes, other assignments, and other plans that perhaps don't include studying calculus.

Or you might find a way of doing the course thing on a subject you like. I spent one summer month in university in an Italian film class. It was awesome. I did it with some film buddies and we sat around a good part of the day watching Fellini movies and then talking about them with an incredibly vivacious professor. It was one of the easiest credits I ever earned, *and* I only had four classes the next semester.

What about doing your last year of English or a credit course in French—in England or France? Yes, there are such things. You could go to another country and take a class that will count here in Canada. And meanwhile you can pop off to Italy on the weekends and do your homework speaking to the butcher rather than one of those lab tapes. By neatly combining course work with travel, you can have your cake and chop off your head too, nicely re-creating Marie Antoinette's last moments right on the actual site. Then you return to Canada, having studied drama at Oxford University and art history at the Louvre, and voilà, that spare thing happens again. Isn't life great when you're a student? They'll even give you a card with your picture on it that says you're a student, and when you're hanging around in other countries people will give you stuff more cheaply just because you're still in school. I love it.

Here's another option that you may think is totally wacko: What about taking a course that you're actually really really interested in, even though it might not give you any credits or anything? It'll let you hang out and do the things you've always wanted to do. Again, my example here is film. There are a ton of hands-on filmmaking courses out there that you could do in the cities that are known for making movies. I couldn't afford the time or money to do a really great six-week program in New York that got you raising money and shooting three movies and all kinds of neat stuff. Instead I did an equally thrilling program at UCLA in California, which for one thing was way cheaper and only a week and a half long, and for another thing I got to shoot my five-minute video on the Universal Studios backlot. And all it cost me was the price of the credit (and, okay, the flight and the accommodations).

There are summer experience courses out there for everything from marine biology to sound recording to astronomy to photography . . . the options are endless. Now I'm not saying that this isn't going to cost you money, because it will. And as I mentioned, I have some ideas on the subject that I'll tell you about later. But for now, consider the possibilities.

## Travelling

Spain! France! Katmandu! Now there are a ton of student travel books out there and I don't have the time or the inclination to tell you where you should go because that's not the kind of book this is. What I do want to do is open you up to the types of travel adventures you could have and why travelling, although it pays you no money and doesn't leave you with anything tangible like a course credit at the end of the summer, could be good for you to do.

Students have been stuffing their backpacks for years now to head off to Europe, Australia, South America, Asia, and wherever else a plane ticket can take them, often with no idea what they're going to do when they get there. What possesses students to do this incredibly weird thing? Well it has a lot to do with removing yourself from the world you're familar with and putting yourself in a place where you don't know the people, customs, traditions, local delicacies, and only a smattering of the language—just to see what happens. What often happens is that you have periods of feeling blue, gross, icky, and depressed, coupled with periods of feeling connected, amazing, alive, and powerful, after which you come home and start taking out the trash without being asked because you're just so grateful that home isn't a hostel any more.

Travelling is about expanding the way you see things, and challenging all your ingrained routines and habits. It's about seeing for yourself what you've only read about in books, and meeting people you never in all your lifetime will ever see again. Once, on a Greek island named Scopolous, I met my soulmates—a bunch of men and women travelling together, only one of whom could really speak any English. It didn't matter. I found them and they found me and thanks to them I know how to dance the country's traditional dance and how to say "Save the turtles" in Greek. I don't think I'll ever see them again, but I'll never forget those two days (and neither will my two travelling companions, who thought I'd been kidnapped by local terrorists).

In the past, companies and corporations have frowned upon the huge chronological gaps in someone's résumé that were spent wandering the globe. But what the business world is beginning to discover is that they actually want the people who've taken the time to go and "find" themselves and to find out about other people; to essentially figure out who they are and what they want, away from all other influences. Often travellers come back with more confidence in handling strange situations, and with a better focus on what's ahead. So travelling may not be justifiable in a concretely productive sense, but it may be the time in your life when you get to sort through some important stuff and take yourself to the next level.

Also possible in the world of travel are special trips and tours that are organized by companies. There are advantages to these. A company may organize a trip so that you can see a country in a special way, or so that you don't have to figure out where to be what day. So instead of backpacking through France, you might want to bike through it with a group. You might go on an organized tour of

Kenya, or see Iceland by ship (while also learning about the environment, but that sounds a lot like a course and maybe you don't want to hear about school any more).

There are also trips that are specifically organized to be hellish so as to help you challenge the way you approach life. Outward Bound courses, for example, are heavy on physical exertion, teamwork, and learning through doing. On Outward Bound you could find yourself travelling through Algonquin Park for twenty-two days, or dogsledding on Baffin Island. You'll bond with a group of strangers and you may spend some time on a "solo," a three-day camp by yourself (with food and water provided).

Your trip could be one week or eight weeks, it could be in your home province or in Africa, and it could be one of many physical challenges—canoeing, rock climbing, sailing, safari. However you design it, it'll be one of the most challenging adventures of your life.

Another way to travel is by giving your time to others. Whether you work with street kids or the elderly, build houses or dig ditches, you can combine the powerful insights of travelling with the warmth of contributing to a community. I know students who've worked all over the world in orphanages, schools, fields, communes, and even with Mother Teresa. Travelling is something that's often very selfish (which can be a good thing), but the whole tone of the trip can change if you choose to dedicate it to someone else's well-being.

## Great, Now How Do I Pay for It?

Good question. You're considering an alternative that doesn't necessarily have parents across Canada standing up and shouting "My child has decided to backpack through Italy rather than get a job. Three cheers for my bright little babe!" No, the cold hard truth is that while some parents will be immediately supportive, most are going to narrow their eyes suspiciously and ask you where the heck you think the money is coming from to be galavanting in the land of pasta. This is the test, which will result in either you starting a screaming match ending with "No one in this house ever wants me to be happy!" and a lot of door-slamming, or your parents remarking on how mature you are, and shouldn't they be giving you a little more freedom. Really.

And here's how: take responsibility for your trip. That means that before you go running to Mom and Dad with a wicked idea that you got out of this book ("I thought I bought you that book so that you could get a job this summer. What is that Schaffer woman telling you?"), you've got some planning to do.

1. Research. How much will your proposed trip cost? Where are you going? Why did you choose where you're choosing? What kinds of things might you do there? Who will you be travelling with? Any kind of proposal and plan of your trip will speak your commitment to going (i.e., this is not just a passing whim) and demonstrate that you have some idea what you're going for (i.e., that you aren't just trying to scam out of working at the hardware store again).

2. Give stuff up. What are you going to sacrifice so that you can go on this trip? Is there something you wanted (like a stereo) that you're willing to put off? Are you willing to work weekends this year to help raise the money you'll need this summer, even if it means you can't go out on Saturday nights? Are you willing to give up some of your freedom to help out more around the house before and after you go? When you've decided that there are things you can sacrifice, you're ready to approach your parents or guardians.

3. Present plans. Ask your parents for a specific time in order to present your proposal. Make them a cup of coffee and sit around the dining room table so that everyone's equal. Make copies of your proposal so that they can see the work you've done. Make it like a business meeting. Ask for questions and comments.

4. Negotiate. If your parents are worried about how much the trip will cost them, tell them that you'll raise money for the trip if they match what you raise. Or if they want you to work this summer, negotiate that you'll work for six weeks and travel for the last two. Or if they still feel strapped for cash, offer to do something around the house that will save them money they could put towards your trip, for instance you could paint the house yourself, or babysit your younger brother. You want to listen to what their biggest concerns are and find ways of addressing those fears instead of getting pissed off. Those fears may be legitimate and you aren't going anywhere until you've found a way for your parents to deal with them. You may even have to negotiate a time period where you help more around the house (say a month), and if they see a marked improvement, they'll help you go travelling.

5. Under no circumstances get angry, whine, or complain. Yelling at your parents is not going to help. If they say no, ask them to wait a week before deciding, or ask them under what circumstances they would say yes (see number four). If they're unsure, don't pester them. Be an adult and you'll get further. Demonstrate your commitment to the trip, but don't get too attatched to their approval of it.

6. If they say yes, keep your promises. This trip can be a major breakthrough in the level of trust and love between you and your parents. If you committed to

doing anything before or after the trip, do it. You may find more rewards in your home life than any trip could provide. Also, keep them involved in your excitement so that they know they made a good choice. You don't have to let them know everything, but share with them a book you're reading on the subject, or a fact you've learned, or a place you want to visit. They'll feel so much a part of your trip that it'll be easier to let you go. When I was in Greece my mother bought a map of the islands. Every time I called her I let her know where I'd been so that she could mark it down on her map. It gave her so much pleasure, and when I came home it made me feel great to tell her stories of what happened in each place and to realize how much she already knew about them.

7. If the answer is still no way, decide if you still want to go. If the trip means a lot to you, you can still go if they say no, it just may not be this summer. Maybe you have to find a job and save the money yourself, even if it takes another year. Like I said, if you're really committed, you'll find a way to go.

So there you have it folks, the Karen Schaffer Method for getting the trip you want and bringing peace, harmony, and love to your home (well, at least this week). A version of this method can also apply to taking courses and volunteering. Good luck, and stay committed.

## Volunteer Work

The first thing that pops into people's heads at the words "volunteer work" are images of kind-faced people in white scurrying around to help people drink stuff through a straw. Or maybe that's my image, 'cause in your image they're wearing blue. Doesn't matter. The point is that the word "volunteer" often conjures up a "do-gooder" image that many of you probably find hard to relate to. Many of us *mean* to volunteer, we really do. We have really good intentions . . . it's just that we're so busy and we need money, and we're thinking "I'm just not a saint," or "I'm not a one-person charity organization, I'm into taking care of me." I've thought all of those thoughts too. But I want you to throw out the idea that volunteer work is about helping other people. It's not about helping other people at all. What volunteer work is really about is getting something for you.

Oh my god, blasphemy! But trust me here, this getting-something-for-you thing doesn't take anything away from the good that you can do in volunteer work. It actually makes you a better volunteer. Let me illustrate this point with a story.

There was a fifteen-year-old student who one summer signed on to be a volunteer at a hospital. The volunteers could work in a number of different departments, and Nita's first assignment was the play area in the children's ward. Now Nita liked children, there was no doubt about that, but as one or two children, maybe three, wandered in and out of the quiet play area, she heard this tiny little voice inside her head saying "Why am I here? This is useless," which of course as we all know is the most horrible thing you could think when you're trying to help poor, sad children in the hospital, even though there were never any regular kids and Nita wasn't sure they even remembered her from the last time.

But being a good volunteer, she squished that horrible thought down and continued—half-heartedly, bored, and definitely guilty—doing her work. Eventually she stopped going. And she felt even worse. Because now she wasn't even with the poor, sad children in the hospital, she was at home, and that made her a truly bad person who must be evil not to want to work with poor, sad children in the hospital, which made her feel even less like showing up for her volunteer duties.

See how doing something to help other people can make you a wreck? Now mind you, Nita was not a bad person. She was just being incredibly human, which is what we all are, and being human she needed some personal stake in what she was doing. What happened was, they changed assignments at the hospital, and Nita started working at the gift shop. Nita was back in business. Now she had a reason for being there because she could learn to use the cash register *so that she could get a job*. Every morning Nita raced over to the hospital to do her volunteer work, racking up those hours on the cash register and waiting for the new *Seventeen* magazines to come in.

Is Nita a bad volunteer for getting something for herself out of her work? No, of course not. It makes her a better volunteer because she's not bored, or half-heartedly trying to pay attention, or beating herself up for being so bored. She's happy and vibrant and chatting to hospital visitors who are trying to decide what gifts to buy for their sick friends and family. Nita is making a difference. Plus, she later got hired at a bookstore because she knew how to work a cash register.

I want you to understand that if you get something for yourself out of the volunteer work you do, *you're actually being a productive and useful volunteer*, with the added bonus that you're happy doing it and that you don't have to beat yourself up for not being so damn saintly. It's called having a stake in doing something. The stake for Nita was that she was going to train herself how to use a cash register and make change. She could contribute to the volunteer program, but she could also take away something that she wanted for herself.

If someone else had been working in the children's ward and their stake had been to get experience with sick children in order to work in home care, or if their stake had been to try out some creative activities to use in their work at an after-four program at school, they wouldn't have approached working in the children's play area the same way. Nita didn't have a stake in working with the children, other than "to help out." It didn't get her very far.

Nor do the stakes have to be job-oriented. Maybe her stake could have been testing out what it would be like to have children of her own. Maybe Nita is often impatient and her stake in doing the children's job would be to teach herself how to be patient. If she ended up being more patient with people in general, that would be something worth volunteering for. Do you see how having a personal stake in something makes a huge difference for the people you're working with, and enables you get something out of doing it? So as I discuss the options in volunteering, think to yourself what you'd like to learn, or train yourself in, or have as experience to get the job you want.

## Volunteering as Do-Gooding (and Doing Good for You, Too)

Volunteering is essentially working without monetary reward for people who benefit from your services. Direct services, wherein you have direct contact with the person you're benefiting, include working with children, the elderly, or the physically disabled. Indirect services, on the other hand, include things like fundraising and office work.

What I define as "traditional" volunteering are the helping services that have to do with non-profit organizations, foundations, charities, and hospitals. You can prepare food in churches or community services (would-be chefs alert) and help to serve it (what a great way to get around "waiting experience only need apply"). You could do office work or translation, accounting, computer, or library work. You could do manual labour, carpentry, painting, or plumbing for seniors homes or community centres, or for individuals and low-income families. You could drive around transporting Meals on Wheels, or take seniors to their medical appointments, or maybe to a movie. If you're thinking you might like to be a doctor, psychologist, or social worker, working in hospitals or addiction clinics could be a great way to discover what you're interested in, or maybe to discover that watching *ER* on TV is as close as you really want to get. You can work in education, as a tutor or helping to teach English; or you can work in communications, helping to write press releases, develop promotional material, and compiling lists of resources.

There are a lot more opportunities, but you can see how much room there is to help out in your community while getting some valuable skills, knowledge, and experience for yourself.

## Charlotte and Me and the Parting of the Red Sea

I myself had done plenty of fundraising and food-drive kind of work, but after my first year of university I realized that I had never done any direct service. My stake was that I wanted to know what it'd be like to work closely with people who needed me, and I challenged myself by choosing an unfamiliar community: the elderly. To me, senior citizens were people I raced by on the street, who have trouble chewing, and who rarely go out (my Grandma didn't count as "elderly," since for one thing she walks faster than I do, and not only does she chew without difficulty but she cooks like a dream, and continues to have a busier social life than my mother and I put together). No matter, I looked upon the elderly as a mysterious Other, who didn't have a lot to do with me.

I made an appointment at the Volunteer Bureau in Montreal (an office that organizes and coordinates volunteers), and got myself an assignment working with the elderly. I both liked and didn't like the work. I spent random days helping out at seniors events, or taking someone to the doctor. It seemed like I was doing a good thing, and I had momentary flashes of pleasure, but I had that same "Why am I bothering?" voice that Nita heard playing around my head every time I was asked to be somewhere. Then I met Charlotte.

Charlotte was then ninety-one years old, and she lived alone in an apartment building near McGill University (where she once used to teach piano, as she told me many times). I originally went to help Charlotte for one day—a nice slow walk to the drugstore. When I say slow, I mean *real* slow. Charlotte had broken her hip the previous year, so my job was to hold her purse (which, if held the wrong way, would spill open) with one arm, and with the other arm I supported her as we took step after step after step, with a pause after each one, until what seemed like days later we'd reach our destination. We walked so slowly that a three-block round-trip literally took us over an hour. When we got back to her apartment I thought I was off the hook. But crafty Charlotte led me to her calender and wouldn't let me leave until she'd booked me to come again. Each time I went Charlotte would make me commit to coming again. If I tried to stall or say no, she'd begin to cry. I was Charlotte's weekly helper for over a year.

Looking back, I had a lot at stake, and I learned so much more than I would have if I'd continued doing the random visits that were already giving me that "I'm a terrible person for not wanting to do this" feeling. Charlotte taught me about commitment. Even when I didn't want to go, I went, and when I could look back and realize that I fulfilled my promise to her for a year, I felt amazing. Further, she taught me a lot about patience. I think, walk, and talk very quickly, and I have a tendency to be impatient with those who can't keep up. With

Charlotte I couldn't move fast or talk fast (she was deaf in one ear anyway and English was her second language), so I just had to hang out. It meant that I really had to listen to her, and it meant that I was really aware of what was happening around me while we were walking down the street. I actually saw someone steal a bike at one of the busiest corners of downtown Montreal. No one saw it but me, because everyone was hurrying by with their eyes elsewhere.

I learned to appreciate my own freedom and mobility. I always loved going places by myself, but now I really understood that being able to run and catch a movie was something to appreciate. And I learned a lot about how people are afraid of the elderly. I'd watch with amazement and embarrassment at how Charlotte would use her elderlyness to get ahead in any lineup. We'd walk into the drugstore and there'd be a lineup of ten people waiting at the prescription counter. Charlotte would start to weave back and forth unsteadily (letting go of my arm and pushing forward all the while) as though she were about to fall over any second. She'd start to shout in this vaguely accented voice, "Hello, hello, can somebody help me please? Are you the doctor that does the prescriptions? I need my medicine. Hello, hello." People would part like the Red Sea so as not to have to deal with the senile old lady

with the pencilled-on eyebrows, and the druggist would come racing to take care of her so that she'd shut up and stop making everyone in the line feel so uncomfortable. I, of course, was initially mortified, and at first I'd say "Charlotte, other people are waiting too," as if I were speaking to a small child. She'd appear not to have heard me (that deaf ear again!) while waving me away with one hand. Eventually I realized that my role was to just stand there and look apologetically helpless, and as a result we always moved to the front of the line in any situation.

I realized how much people in our society don't want to be confronted by the reality of being old, and how much that separated them from human beings like Charlotte: full of mischief, merriment, and manipulation, as well as wisdom and humour. I might have helped Charlotte get her epsom salts and vitaman C, but she gave me a lot more.

## Volunteer Work as Work Experience (Yes, it Counts)

So that's one version of how to do volunteer work. The other version still has you providing services to people who benefit, but the stake that you have in volunteering is a little more apparent. Volunteering, or interning, is an excellent way to get experience at any kind of job, and to make connections. It's another way of generating contacts, like we talked about in Chapter 5.

There are many examples of this. My editor on this book got started by volunteering at the Women's Press. Among the other small things that volunteers end up doing, Karen was able to do her first real proofreading and production work. This gave her a chance to get a feel for working in a publishing house, and how to handle herself in that environment.

Back in the days when I was interested in film I volunteered on a community cable service show. It wasn't a grandiose project, but every Sunday I'd help to create and dismantle the set, set the lights, and work a camera. For those of you who think that only contacts can get you that kind of experience, I mention this job because I didn't really know anybody, just another student who told me about it. Eight months later when I was done, I had on-set experience and a letter of recommendation from the director and creator of the program.

Volunteering can advance your career by getting you experience and connections that will get you hired the next summer. Many students started the great jobs they have now by volunteering or interning for a summer first and then getting hired back based on their performance. If you have any wish to be hired in the future, you have to do a stellar job as a volunteer now. That means taking initiative, and doing all that's asked of you without complaint.

However, there are limits. It's okay to work really hard on a volunteer job you love, but if the company doesn't treat you well, or refuses to hire you after an extended length of time, you need to take care of yourself. Think of it this way: you're volunteering to gain experience. Once you've been there for a summer, you're probably now experienced. If a company is trying to get you to work for them two or three summers in a row without paying you for a job you know and are qualified to do, get out.

Lastly, you can do volunteer work just for the sheer fun of it. I know a student who volunteered one day a week at a theatre so that he could see all the plays for free. I also have two friends who every year volunteer to be waiters at a big charity event because for them it's the most fun way to spend the evening.

## Okay You Sold Me, So Now What?

If you like the idea of volunteering, here's what you can expect. First of all, the organization should give you tasks suited to your training and experience. You should be able to get a precise description of your duties and your role in the organization or job. You should be informed of your schedule, and get any training you need in order to handle whatever situations you may encounter. You should be treated with respect.

By the same token, you're expected to be open and honest about your motivations and goals. That will actually get you placed the most usefully for both you and the organization. You're expected to understand the job before accepting it, do any necessary training, carry out the tasks assigned, and let your supervisor know as soon as possible if you can't do what you've said. Just because you're not getting paid doesn't mean you haven't made a commitment.

# Run Your Own Business

Last idea of the day. This alternative to the get-a-job route is actually also a job. I considered creating another job chapter called "Working with Yourself," but for one thing I can't promise that you'll make any money, and for another thing I wanted some time to chat about it with you outside the job guide format. I'm going to speak to those of you who live at home and only need to make extra cash, but I'm also going to give some examples of bigger projects that spun off into companies and actual full-time businesses. So if you're at university and the money from dogwalking just won't cut it any more, hang in there 'cause I'll be addressing possibilities for you too.

If you've got an entrepreneurial spirit, a vision, or a downright hard-nosed practical business sense, you may want to consider running your own business. Now if you've just decided that this isn't for you because when I said "practical business sense" you envisioned yourself holed up in some insanely small office surrounded by a mound of papers trying to make the rent and doing who knows what because you don't know how to do anything anyway, STOP. Having your own business doesn't necessarily mean that you need a lot of capital (money to start with) or overhead (fixed costs, like rent, that can sink a little business fast). Most of the businesses I'm going to suggest are ones that you can totally handle for a summer.

First things first: most of us have already been entrepreneurs. Have you ever babysat before? In that case you were working for yourself. Other people came to you for help, and you were your own mini-business. When Mrs. Schelickinheimer down the street called you up to ask if you could sit for her next Friday, you checked your book before you said yes, didn't you? (You may have also had to check with your mother, but who's being picky?) You were, at some level, being your own boss.

Some of the things you can do in your own neighbourhood require only that you be pretty decent at it and motivated to find your own clientele. Number one basic idea is being a dogwalker or sitter, a housesitter, or a babysitter. Dog-walking or sitting is an easy business to start if you live around people with dogs. I know someone who pays her eleven-year-old neighbour twelve bucks a week to come in three times a day to look in on their new puppy and take him out for a midday bathroom break. A housesitter may be someone who comes in to water the plants and collect the mail. Those of you who are older may have the chance to actually stay in the place you're housesitting (number one way to get around that pesky rent problem). And of course babysitting, as every teenager's standby job, can be a boon for extra cash. Have you ever heard of the Babysitters Club? (Stay with me here, even you cynical people.) It's a series of books about these girls who start a babysitting service in their neighbourhood. Whether you adore the books or not, think about the initiative in that project. Having one central phone line where neighbourhood parents would be sure of getting a booking is a pretty good idea. That's taking an old standby and finding a way to improve on it to generate more work. So those of you in the "extra spending money only" category can think about ways to make some of these old ideas fresher.

Next is the odd-job category of job creation. I know students who've had their own driveway sealing, roofing, and painting businesses. If you have any construction or repair skills, you can offer your services for less than what a professional company would charge. I know a guy who started a painting company in university.

It's now four years later and his company has expanded to include carpet cleaning and other household needs, and he continues to manage and own the company full time. Interestingly enough, this wasn't his first venture. In high school he started a tie-dye shirt company (when that was the craze), and had his brothers and sisters down in the basement helping him figure out how to create amazing patterns and colours on white cotton shirts. Practising with that business first, Peter was able to parlay his knowledge into his painting business.

If you don't have advanced construction or repair skills you could approach people for jobs you can handle. An actor friend of mine got himself through some tight spots by working as a general handyperson. Think about this: in every household there are about three jobs that the people living there keep meaning to do but never have the time, or keep forgetting to get the right screws for, or aren't sure how to do. You can get yourself work at various homes doing those kind of chores. So at one house you build a composter, hang a mirror, and clean the garage. At the next house you paint the eavestroughs, alphabetize the books, and re-organize the attic. These things could take you a day or a week, and you could charge by the hour or create a flat rate for each job. You'll have to do a lot of self-promotion, and get your previous customers to recommend you to others, but you could keep yourself going for a summer doing this type of work.

The other favourite neighbourhood jobs are lawn mowing, leaf raking, and snow shovelling. These seasonal jobs are great, particularly lawn mowing, because it taps into everyone's laziness (who really wants to spend their weekend cutting the lawn?) and that beautiful grass just keeps on growing. One student I know, Gian, had a lawn cutting business he inherited (actually he bought it) from his brothers. They'd developed the business, and already had a base of regular summer customers. Gian spent a summer managing the business and helping it to expand. He used some of the money he made to get a high-powered (faster) lawn mower and he hired his sister to help him out. Now Gian is a pretty savvy guy, and like all good owners he realized that he didn't even necessarily have to be there to have this business run. So he turned the managing part over to a friend and spent the summer in an immersion camp in Quebec. When the next summer rolled around Gian again decided that the lawn care business would be okay without him. So he went off to be a camp counsellor, raking in the profits while his buddy sweated away over power motors. When Gian went to university he sold the business to his brother (for a profit of course). He later sold it to some neighbours, who then ran it into the ground, but Gian walked away free and clear, both owning a business and getting to do other things as well. And making money. You too can exploit your family and friends. And they don't mind 'cause they've got a job.

You may also want to try running your own store. One student ran a sarong and shirt stand in Ontario cottage country for a summer, and hired her brother and cousin to help (notice how your family make excellent employees?). I don't think they made a whole lot of money in the end, but they did learn how to manage a retail operation.

If for whatever reason you've got access to a store space or a stand there are all kinds of things you could sell. You need to pick things that you can get in stock quickly (you only have the summer full time after all) and that you can cover the cost of (don't have a furniture store that'll leave you high and dry come the end of August). I know students who've run craft stands and made things like hats and aprons to sell. Also, you may find that you can get a job selling a product that a company will provide. (Remember that you can get scammed here, so you don't want to be putting huge money up front, and you do want to be checking the company out with the Better Business Bureau.) I know two students who sold backyard play equipment for a summer. They learned all about the products from the guy who made them, and then they went out and did a lot of advertising. When they got a sale, they'd pick up the equipment and assemble it for the parent in the yard. For that they'd get a huge cut of the sale. If they were to make any money, it was up to them to do the work.

You can learn so much by having any version of your own business. One of the things I learned was how to set my fees. When I started doing résumés for people as a business, I charged a ridiculously low fee to start. Everyone who came to me was vaguely suspicious of whether I knew what I was talking about, and whether the résumés would work. Strangely, the more I raised my fees, the less people questioned my ability. Now I'm sure that my time and expertise is worth a lot of money (and you can bet the price is going up again now that this book is out). You have to have confidence in your abilities so that people will want to hire you, and that means charging the going rates.

I've given you some options to think about. You may look around your own neighbourhood or city and see a need that isn't being met and that you could fill. That's where to start. If you need seed money, try getting a loan from a government venture program, or see if you can convince some people to become your investors. Once you've picked the project, the real work starts. You need organization and planning. In the bibliography at the end of this book, I recommend one called *Start and Run a Profitable Student-Run Business* by David Schincariol. This book is a gold mine for those of you with good ideas. It has business plans, checklists, and lots of good advice. So go for it . . . and if you don't make any money, who cares? It looks great on a résumé!

## You've Only Just Begun . . .

There you have it boys and girls, alternatives to actually getting a job. The wild thing is that these options can end up paying off down the line in ways you never expected. Some people end up making careers out of what they started to do for fun. Don't give up exploring your options, especially this early in the game. There's no one better to employ as an adult than a person who's richer for their experiences, and who's confident in their choices because they've explored some different avenues.

So here we are at the end of the book, and now I really have to go and leave you to it. I've talked about a lot of things, but none is so important as acknowledging where you are. I know there are a lot of pressures out there and inside yourself for you to be responsible and get a job and make money and have some sort of purpose when you get out of bed in the morning. That's human. The thing we sometimes miss as humans is that the process of it all is just as important as the end goal. Horrible as it is, the yucky "I don't have a job" feeling is just as crucial to your life as getting a job.

I've recently taken up yoga. After one of my first classes, I went up to my teacher and told her that I was afraid I'd pulled my back in a particular posture. She looked at me, smiled, and said, "You can't get hurt here." She must have read my look of disbelief because she continued, "The only way you get hurt is by resisting. Surrender yourself to the movement. Don't worry about how far you can stretch—where you are is exactly where you're supposed to be." And you know what? It turned out I hadn't pulled anything in my back after all.

I know that each and every one of you is amazing and has something to contribute to any job situation. But whether you get the job or not, you're still okay. Where you are is exactly where you're supposed to be. I'm a bit nervous because as I finish this, I'm going to have to start something new too. So wherever you are, I'm going through it with you. Good luck and powerful job hunting. . . .

Karen

# APPENDIX

# Skills You Never Knew You Had

I compiled these two lists of skills in order to help you get your juices flowing when you're composing your résumé, cover letters, and interview answers. Think about how these words might apply to your experiences and attributes. They'll help you articulate just who you are, what you've done, and how you did it. (And here you were thinking they were just verbs and adjectives.)

## Functional Skills

Achieved
Acquired
Activated
Adjusted
Administered
Analyzed
Applied
Appraised
Arranged
Assembled
Assigned
Attained
Authorized
Bought
Budgeted
Built
Catalogued
Classified
Co-ordinated
Coached
Communicated
Compared
Composed
Complied
Computed/calculated
Conceived
Conducted
Constructed
Consulted
Controlled
Counselled
Created
Dealt with
Debated
Decided
Defined
Delegated
Designed
Developed
Diagnosed
Directed
Empowered
Encouraged
Enlisted
Established
Estimated
Evaluated
Examined
Exceeded
Executed
Expanded
Expedited
Explained
Facilitated
Figured out
Finalized
Followed up/through
Forecasted
Foresaw
Formulated
Fostered(relationships)
Generated
Guarded
Guided

Headed
Helped
Hired
Implemented
Improved
Increased
Indexed
Influenced
Informed
Initiated
Inspected
Installed
Instructed
Interpreted
Interviewed
Invented
Investigated
Judged
Launched
Learned
Led
Listened
Maintained
Managed
Manipulated
Mechanized
Mediated
Memorized
Merged
Modulated
Monitored
Motivated
Moulded
Negotiated
Observed
Organized
Oversaw
Participated
Perceived
Performed
Persuaded
Planned
Prepared
Presented
Presided
Prioritized
Problem-solved
Produced
Programmed
Projected
Promoted
Questioned
Recognized
Recommended
Reconciled
Recruited
Rectified
Reduced
Released
Rendered
Renegotiated
Renovated
Reorganized
Repaired
Reported
Researched
Reviewed
Revised
Saved
Scheduled
Selected
Serviced
Set up
Sold
Sorted (out)
Stimulated
Straightened
Summarized
Supervised
Synthesized
Systematized
Taught
Tended
Trained
Translated
Trouble-shoot
Uncovered
Unravelled
Utilized
Verified
Viewed
Wrote

## Personality Skills

Adaptable
Adventurous
Aggressive
Ambitious
Affable
Assertive
Boastful
Calm
Cautious
Competitive
Confident
Co-operative
Curious
Decisive
Dominant
Easygoing
Efficient
Empathetic
Energetic
Enthusiastic
Firm
Flexible
Funny
Fussy
Humorous
Idealistic
Imaginative
Independent
Intuitive
Inventive
Loyal
Moody
Opportunistic
Optimistic
Organized
Outspoken
Patient
Persistent
Planful
Practical
Praising
Respectful
Responsible
Relaxed
Sarcastic
Serious
Sociable
Spendthrift
Systematic
Tactful
Talkative
Tolerant
Tough
Trusting

## Books that I Used and Liked (or Books You Could Use to Find Out More about Stuff I Didn't Cover)

*The 1997 Canada Student Employment Guide: The Definitive Tool for a Successful Job Search in Canada*, by Kevin Makra, Student Employment Network, Toronto, Ont. To order call (416) 971-5090.

*The Canadian Guide to Working and Living Overseas: For Entry-Level and Seasoned Professionals*, Jean-Marc Hachy, Intercultural Systems/Systèmes Interculturels (ISSI), Ottawa, 1992.

*Careers for:*

- *Sports Nuts and Other Athletic Types*
- *Film Buffs*
- *Gourmets*
- *Number Crunchers*
- *Good Samaritans*
- *Bookworms*
- *Computer Buffs*
- *Animal Lovers*
- *Environmental Types*
- *Crafty People*
- *Culture Lovers*
- *Foreign Language Afficionados*
- *Kids at Heart*
- *Nature Lovers*
- *Travel Buffs*

Lincolnwood, Illinois: VGM Career Horizons, a division of NTC Publishing Group, 1994.

*Get Wired, You're Hired*, by Mark Swartz, Scarborough, Ont.: Prentice Hall Canada, 1997.

*Start and Run a Profitable Student-Run Business: Your Step-by-Step Plan for Turning Bright Ideas into Big Bucks*, by David Schincariol, Vancouver, B.C.: Self-Counsel Press Ltd., 1995.

*Strategy of the Dolphin: Scoring a Win in a Chaotic World*, by Dudley Lynch and Paul L. Kordis, New York: Ballantine Books, 1988.